MASTERING THE SHAKESPEARE AUDITION

MASTERING THE SHAKESPEARE AUDITION

A Quick Guide to Performance Success

DONNA SOTO-MORETTINI

Bloomsbury Methuen Drama
An imprint of Bloomsbury Publishing Plc

B L O O M S B U R Y
LONDON · OXFORD · NEW YORK · NEW DELHI · SYDNEY

Bloomsbury Methuen Drama

An imprint of Bloomsbury Publishing Plc

50 Bedford Square	1385 Broadway
London	New York
WC1B 3DP	NY 10018
UK	USA

www.bloomsbury.com

Bloomsbury is a registered trade mark of Bloomsbury Publishing Plc

First published 2016

Copyright © Donna Soto-Morettini 2016

British Library Cataloguing-in-Publication Data
A catalogue record for this book is available from the British Library.

ISBN: PB: 978-1-4742-6685-7
ePDF: 978-1-4742-6687-1
ePub: 978-1-4742-6686-4

Library of Congress Cataloging-in-Publication Data
A catalog record for this book is available from the Library of Congress.

Cover design: Hugh Cowling
Cover image © National Portrait Gallery

Typeset by Fakenham Prepress Solutions, Fakenham, Norfolk NR21 8NN

CONTENTS

ACKNOWLEDGEMENTS

Thanks to my colleagues Iain Davie, Ian Dunn, Martin Lowe and Lise Olson for discussing early ideas and offering their wisdom. Thanks to Paul Harper-Swan for providing a workshop and some wonderful actors – Gayle Telfer Stevens, Natalie Toyne, Eric Robertson, Joanne McGuinness, Karen Fishwick, Pamela Byrne, Kieran Baker, Tom Duncan and Gavin Paul – for workshopping in the early phases of my explorations. Thanks to Anna Vanosi and to all the students at Edinburgh Napier University, who happily take on new ideas, explore new ways of working and always report back with grace and good humour.

Picture credits

PREFACE

It obviously cannot be that there is a shortage of books about Shakespeare. I picked up a recent volume of Shakespeare Quarterly and find that the bibliography for 1997 contains 4780 items, 342 of which are about Hamlet: *almost one a day. What sort of thing do the authors of these items find to say?*

— FRANK KERMODE[1]

You simply wouldn't think that there might be room for another book on Shakespeare. Surely he is the most written-about author of all time and reading Frank Kermode's words above should be enough to put anyone off the attempt.

But after many, many years of teaching young actors I have at length come to a conclusion that will surprise many: there does seem to be a gap in the Shakespeare market! Having taught classical acting, and Shakespeare in particular, in some of Britain's leading conservatoires I have – like most of my colleagues – relied heavily on a few books to help ease beginning actors into the technical and emotional challenges of bringing his work to life on stage. I know that I am not alone in supplying aspiring actors with a recommended reading list that includes works by Cicely Berry, Barbara Houseman, Patsy Rodenberg, Peter Hall, John Barton and, recently, Giles Block and David and Rebecca Carey. We recommend these books because they're great works, written by people who have many years' experience with actors and with Shakespeare.

---

[1] 'Writing About Shakespeare', *London Review of Books*, Vol. 21, No. 24, 9 December 1999.

But these books – wonderful as they are – begin at a point that, for many young actors, feels a bit advanced. They assume, for the most part, that the reader has found a way to make sense of Shakespeare's text and, again, for the most part, they assume that the reader has had some practical experience with Shakespeare. But more than that, they focus largely on approaching the language in the context of the play and not on the very specifically demanding art of using Shakespeare's text for an audition.

I find that most actors develop a real love of working with Shakespeare, but very few of them start with that feeling. Instead, they begin with fear and also with a very strong sense that there is a RIGHT way to perform *Hamlet* or *Lady Macbeth* and that whatever that RIGHT way is, they just don't know it.

As I was beginning this book, I saw a documentary on the BBC called *Muse of Fire*, which featured interviews with many well-known and experienced actors, talking about their early experiences of working with Shakespeare. All of them spoke very frankly about the fear that his work inspired in them. The documentary was an interesting study in just how scary even great actors find the work when they first begin.

My idea here is to focus very specifically on one particular kind of Shakespeare performance: the monologue. More specifically yet, this book is going to focus on preparing and performing a Shakespeare monologue for audition. I hope, however, that the book will have broader application and that it will prove helpful to many in their general Shakespeare preparations as well.

In the life of an actor, the requirement to prepare a Shakespeare monologue generally only comes up at two points: at the drama school audition point and at the point of auditioning for live theatre where artistic directors are planning on some classical work in their repertory season. In my years of working with actors of all ages and experience, I have seen that the Shakespeare monologue remains a pretty daunting task. I've coached many who have been out of drama school and working professionally for years, but feel quite intimidated by the idea of preparing a classical monologue. Some of those I've worked with were facing an audition after many years of doing television work or musical theatre and feeling very far away from the kind of 'second year Shakespeare' production they did in drama school. Some have found themselves cast in contemporary drama for most of their working careers and suddenly feel unsure about the process of tackling heightened language. I hope this book will prove helpful for them, as well as for many young actors at the beginning and at the end of their training.

INTRODUCTION

Turning the whole process on its head

2 HOURS

The chances are you are reading this because you are looking for some help with an upcoming audition. But there's a great difference between the reader who knows that they will have auditions coming up in a few months and the reader who has an audition in two weeks. So, critically, we are going to talk about time all the way through this guide – partly because when you have to do an audition next week (or even the week after that) time is of the essence. It is my belief that, if you prepare in the right way, you can perform a monologue with confidence in 30 to 35 hours.

Most actors feel so hampered by their combined fears of doing Shakespeare and doing an audition that they feel they never get to the point where an audition panel can see what they're truly capable of. But if you can find 35 hours of focused time between reading this and doing your audition, I promise you will feel more confident in the audition than you have before. Thirty-five hours of focused concentration is what it is going to take to get you to walk into the audition room and have a very real sense of what to do and how to do it. I can't promise to make you a great actor in 35 hours, but this process will allow you to be the best actor you can be right now when you go into that audition room.

Along with targeting those who have an audition coming up within the month, my challenge in writing this book is to help deepen knowledge and confidence for people who *aren't* under the tremendous time pressure of having a monologue to prepare for audition in the next few weeks, so I'll also include a lot of information that will serve that purpose. Throughout the book it will be very clear what to do if you need to prepare quickly. In order to stay within our 35 hours, you will find estimated timings on everything here, including reading this introduction and doing all the exercises described. That means you can plan your rehearsals carefully prior to your audition.

This book is aimed squarely at preparing Shakespeare monologues for audition. But one can hardly do that without taking other things into consideration along the way. To do any Shakespeare monologue well, an actor has to speak the language with confidence and expressivity. They must be confident about the way the monologue is structured; confident about meaning and confident about who they're talking to and what they're trying to achieve.

The book works by guiding you through a series of creative ways to engage with the text of a monologue. In these engagements, we'll be guided by recent research into the best ways to learn and into how the brain works. We'll be engaging both focused and diffused modes of thinking and we'll be creating powerful memory retrieval cues. The aim in this series of 'creative engagements' is two-fold: first, they will help you feel that the monologue preparation happens in a rather organic way: there should be no forced memorization, no stress and no sense of disconnection between your heart and the text. Second, they are aimed at helping you to externalize your thoughts and actions and to ensure that you are utilizing different parts of the brain for preparation and for memory retrieval. By relying on visual and motor cortex areas of the brain, we significantly increase our powers of memorization and that, in turn, boosts our ability to engage in the world of the monologue we are performing.

Most actors have experienced the way that auditions can increase self-consciousness. Without the aid of a company of players, weeks of rehearsal, lights, set, costume, the sheer 'aloneness' of auditioning seems to amplify our awareness of ourselves. We 'review' our performance as we go along, we become aware of trying to think ahead to the next line, we try to force ourselves to relive the emotion that seemed so right in our bedroom rehearsal. Our only defence against this crippling self-consciousness is to make certain that text retrieval is 'automatic', to give ourselves a strong sense of an external imagined world, and to allow ourselves to inhabit that world fully. Everything we'll be doing here is aimed at helping you create those conditions. In order to achieve all this, we will work in three phases:

Phase 1 – This is where you concentrate on acquiring the tools you'll need. **You can't skip this section, because you will need every one of these tools, but the exact time it should take to complete the minimum of work will be clear and is part of your 35 hours prep.** The good news, however, is that you will only ever have to read this introduction and do Phase 1 ONCE. These two sections take roughly 13 hours. So, if you prepare a second monologue, or a third, the time needed will reduce to only 22 hours.

Phase 2 – In this phase, you will concentrate on choosing and preparing a monologue. This section will help you discover monologues that will play to your strengths, help you get over the fear of handing verse and help you to prepare the text. Don't be fooled by the word 'preparation' though. In this case, all the preparation is actually the foundational phase of rehearsal: it is where we learn to identify the through-line of action in a piece, get a clear picture of structure and also where we create a detailed world of the monologue.

Phase 3 – this is the shortest phase: a step-by-step guide to rehearsal for performance.

All three phases are linked, because the final phase requires the skills and knowledge gained in the first two – so don't be tempted to skip to the end, as it won't be possible for you to do that. But you will be able to plan your time wisely, as all three phases clearly indicate the minimum amount of time you need to spend in each exercise.

For those who aren't under time pressure, there will be more examples and exercises in the last section of the book, which are designed to help you feel confident in your understanding.

This book is, by the nature of its aims, concise and to the point. It includes a lot of exercises that reinforce ideas presented and also gives you some powerful tools in unlocking the multiple meanings that you may find in Shakespeare's work. Throughout the 35-hour journey, you may find that the methods I present here are very different from your usual working method. But I promise you will ultimately finish this work feeling much more confident in Shakespeare's company.

A different way of working

I might as well be very upfront with this: the method here is going to feel pretty foreign. If you've done any acting at all – whether that is just in your acting class at school or you have three years of training at a conservatoire – you are probably going to find my approach somewhat counter-intuitive.

After many years of working with and talking to actors, I know that the usual 'prep' for most of them goes something like this:

- Finding and trying out the parts of the monologue that have some emotional resonance for them and having a go at a couple of emotionally charged read-throughs.

- Moving on quickly to some hard 'rote' memorization sessions in which they attempt to 'get off book'.

- Reading some of the critical notes (with a good edition) and looking up words that aren't immediately decipherable.

- Rehearsing the monologue with 'feeling'.

- (After enough clarity about the language, enough rote-learning and enough emotionally charged readings), the actor confronts an audition panel and hopes for the best.

Over the years I've asked many actors to describe their preparation process and, while most do a version of the points listed above, some add others things: recording their own voices and listening back, writing out monologues in their own hand, doing everything 'backward', putting everything into their own language, playing opposite intentions – I've heard all of these as possible preparation techniques. Of course, these are all ways of engaging with the text, but I think we can find better, stronger methods. I think what actors need in preparation is a powerful understanding of how a speech is structured, where the action is and where all the clues are to help your understanding. Recording yourself won't help you with that. Writing out a monologue won't help you with that and getting emotionally involved won't help you either.

When actors feel these kinds of methods have been successful, they are usually basing those judgements on the sense that the acting felt good to them, that it was all 'clicking' and that they were able to remember the monologue without difficulty. But I find that it is pretty rare for actors to feel that they have done the monologue well, or as well as they could have, in audition and I think that sense of 'underachieving' comes down to preparation. The way that we are going to prepare will almost certainly be different for you. I've spent many years teaching this approach and I have never yet had an actor tell me that it didn't work better for him or her than what he or she was doing before. So perhaps, whatever your misgivings about letting all of your usual preparation go, you might want to give the unorthodox approach presented here a chance. After all, you can always go back to what you were doing before!

For most actors who come to his work for the first time, Shakespeare is a puzzle. But, as actors, we clearly WANT ways to play with this extraordinary, challenging, beautiful puzzle and I'm hoping that you will keep that idea in mind as we work. The series of creative engagements in this book represent ways of playing with a (possibly puzzling) monologue that will help you get inside its structure and its meaning and then begin to create the world in which it is set. Some of these approaches might feel familiar, but many won't and that will probably depend on your experience. But whatever your experience, there are some important things to remember as we work.

As outlined above, if you are doing this for the first time, we are going to work in three phases. When doing the first two phases you <u>must</u> be willing to let go of:

- your desire to act
- your desire to memorize
- your desire to 'get into' character
- your desire to emote
- your desire to go back to any of your old habits

This is critical. You must feel that you can absolutely concentrate on the technical things that we are going to be looking at first without involving emotion, psychology, character 'description', actions, intentions, or ANY of the things you usually bring to your acting.

I realize that this probably feels counter-intuitive – and for much of my career I have counselled actors always to keep technique and imagination securely coupled, so the idea of turning that on its head is foreign even to me. However, when it comes to preparing Shakespeare, I've learned that giving in to our desire to act from the start places some serious limitations on what we can do with the work. These limitations come from two things:

1 **Goal-oriented language can sound dull**

   Most actors use the language of intention or action when preparing a role. In other words, they (quite rightly) ask themselves: what does this character want? What does this character do to achieve what they want? How does this character have to make other people feel in order to get what they want? These questions lead to active choices and are an important part of the actor's process. But they also mean that the actor grows very goal-oriented: I must do this in order to get that. In many cases, it means that the actor has a very direct action in mind and I often find these things written alongside the actor's rehearsal text. It is that very directness that often causes a kind of 'collapse' in the range of our vocal sound. You can test this for yourself by thinking of the ways in which your sound differs when speaking directly about something you need or want ('Please give me those keys' or 'Don't tell me what to do') and when you are speaking more speculatively or descriptively about something that is not connected to an action ('I wonder what would happen if I just walked over and kissed him?' or 'The sky was incredibly blue and vast and everywhere I could hear bees humming and birds singing'). For most people, these 'non-action-based' sentences have a bit more variation in sound than the first set of sentences do. It is the irony of the actor's process: often in our desire to be specific and active, our speech sound can become too direct and too dull.

2 **We equate 'conversational' sound with 'truthful' acting**

   When we first encounter a monologue, we often attempt to place ourselves in a kind of 'conversational' mode of speech. This is the mode of speech that feels natural for us; therefore many actors equate that 'conversational' sound with BEING natural. Most actors spend the majority of their time working on contemporary scripts, either for stage or screen and they concentrate on making those scripts sound natural. Because we see far more film and television acting than stage acting (and certainly we see film and television far more frequently than we see live Shakespeare productions), our ears tune themselves to small and limited vocal choices. We start thinking that these small and limited vocal choices feel 'natural' and, therefore, believable to both ourselves and to our audience. In fact, for most young actors, the idea of using their voice in big, bold ways almost always results in them feeling like they're being 'hammy' or 'over the top'. Yet Shakespeare's texts require much more than dull and direct speech and much more than a 'conversational sound'. They require resonance, dimension, range and expressivity, but, above all, they require clarity – and in order to achieve that we need to explore sound initially without placing any limitations on ourselves.

The final reason for resisting our desire to act or engage our psycho-logically rooted reading too early in the process is that actors often get trapped into an interpretation that prevents them from discovering other (perhaps more exciting) possibilities that emerge when attending to the technical sounds and structures of the text first. Shakespeare left a lot of clues for actors in sounds and structure and when you learn how to discover them, you'll be grateful that you weren't already locked into your acting choices.

It will probably be difficult to let go of your habits, but you must try. You will get back to acting in Phase 3 and, when you do, you will not only be much better prepared, you will find that the 'acting' part feels grounded and organic.

The particular fear of performing Shakespeare

I have just done a rough calculation of how many Shakespeare monologues I've heard in auditions over the span of my career so far. I won't bore you with the maths, but I think it comes to well over 8,000.[1] You learn quite a lot after all those experiences, even if you weren't particularly expecting to. But perhaps the most important things I've learned have had to do with the level of fear that the Shakespeare monologue and Shakespeare's language inspires in most actors.

There are many things that frighten us: spiders, heights, wide open spaces, small enclosed spaces, death, the loss of a loved one, but whatever it is we fear, there are only two things that can lessen that fear: knowledge and experience. I'm not suggesting for a minute that knowledge and experience will dismantle fear – far from it. They can, however, lessen fear in most cases – and increased familiarity with anything can take some of the edge off of fear.

I'm going to try to tackle the fear of Shakespeare; of his language, of the 'rules' of performing Shakespeare; and the fear of doing Shakespeare monologues in this book. I'm going to try to do that in the most efficient, simple and straightforward way that I can. But in order for you to get the most out of all this, you'll need to try to let go of some of your fear – especially the three fears I most often encounter: fear of getting it wrong, fear of being a 'hammy' actor and the fear of not knowing where to start.

1. 'I'm afraid I'll get it wrong'

I hear this often when I'm working with actors, but if you've carefully prepared and spent the recommended amount of time here on your preparation, you can't be wrong.

You can be dull. You can be irritating. You can be too quiet. You can be fake. You can be emotionally rather empty. You can be fuzzy and unspecific.

---

[1] I *knew* there would someone who wanted the maths. At Central, we held auditions seven months out of the year. I did first round auditions every other week, at which we saw thirty-five candidates. That's seventy per month, times seven (490). We did five recall days a year with fifty people recalled each time and asked them to learn a different monologue. That's another 250 (or 740 all together). I did this for five years at Central (3,700) and for seven years at LIPA (8,880 altogether). I auditioned less at the Royal Conservatoire and less at Edinburgh Napier, but easily saw another 700 Shakespeare audition monologues over my years at the RCS and 300 at Edinburgh Napier, so approximately 9,880. Of course this doesn't count the number of monologues I see in master classes and regular classes which would no doubt bring the total closer to 10K …

But you can't be wrong. **This applies not only to your audition monologue as you perform it, but also to your preparation work in this book**.

As long as you've read through each section and you understand what you are trying to do, you can't be WRONG. For every exercise, I've provided a couple of different ways to do them in the 'sample' sections – but we are not talking about science here. We are talking about ART. And art means never having to say you are wrong.

But, of course, art also means ALWAYS having to say you are prepared and that you've put many hours into that preparation. Art also means bringing your passion to whatever it is you do.

You won't find out exactly how to connect your heart with performance in this book. You won't find out how to do that in ANY book. But if you start with curiosity and some ability to empathize with others, with a little work you'll get better and better at finding out just how well you can express what's in your heart through Shakespeare's incredible words.

2. I'm afraid of being too 'hammy' or 'over the top'

We've looked briefly at how quieter, mumbled sounds can sometimes feel 'natural' and 'conversational' to actors and we know that these sounds aren't adequate to the task we are going to be attempting here. That means we need to work on getting comfortable with making bigger, bolder, more expressive vocal choices when we work on this heightened text.

Before we give in to this fear, however, we need to ask what 'hammy' or 'over the top' means. Is it possible to be 'hammy' if you are working with what feels truthful to you and that which feels connected to the imagined world of the text around you? I have seen actors make extraordinarily big choices, but they weren't 'over the top' because the actor had such a strong sense of belief in what they were doing. This means that your real fear isn't about being big, or 'over the top' – it is about not being able to believe in yourself or in your imagined world.

The more we work with bigger sounds and the more we strengthen the sense of our imagined world, the less powerful this fear will feel for you.

3. 'I don't know where to start with Shakespeare'

This is the third most common worry I hear when working with actors and it is also the main reason why most actors simply throw themselves into an emotionally charged reading of a monologue from the start and then follow that up with a couple of hours of trying to cram the piece into their memory.

I promise you that once you work your way through this book, you'll have a lot of ideas and a lot of tools to employ in the process of preparing and performing a Shakespeare audition and you'll grow more comfortable with the idea of leaving emotion and rote memorization aside in the early phases of the work.

To that end, we'll be using some powerful weapons that will take us right to heart of what each monologue is about, how it is structured, what kinds of expressive sounds we have at our disposal and what kinds of clues to meaning and action lie buried within the text itself. Once we done all that work, we'll be ready to play.

Once you let go of these fears and get through all our preparatory work, your final job is to enjoy playing.

Shakespeare wrote plays, yes?

And you can't play with the big ideas and the big passions that he wrote about, if you are worrying about being wrong or 'over the top'. Because no one wrote more playfully, more passionately, more enjoyably for an actor than he did. So, although we are going to start with some technical things (the mastery of which will set us free), the job you have, once we begin the acting part, is simply to play – the way you did when you were a child.

Remember that feeling? The one you had when you were younger and you decided to be a detective? Or a bank robber? Or a monster? You just did it, didn't you? You just threw yourself into that world and pretended that ***it really did exist***. That's all you need to do in the later phases of experiment and exploration here. Remember that feeling of playing with abandon. Without being judged. Just throwing yourself in at the deep end of imagination and enjoying the feeling of exercising every creative muscle you have.

There's a reason it is important to keep this in mind while you are working and it is this: The dullest, most uninspiring Shakespeare performances that I see are almost always the

result of the performer worrying that they will get Shakespeare wrong. You might just have to trust me if what I'm about to say feels counter-intuitive BUT – it is much better to put your heart into risking your quirky, one-of-a-kind interpretation in a bold way than it is to be careful and worried about being wrong...

How to use this book

You will note that every section is timed and that the timings are fairly general because some people work very quickly and some take more time. Testing the material in workshops has allowed me to come to an average time that should be workable for most people, erring on the slow side. This means that if you are a very fast worker/reader, you will almost certainly have extra time. Don't concentrate too much on that – just make sure that you do every exercise as described.

Of course, no one can do 35 hours consecutively – it would result in sleep deprivation and bad learning. Ideally, the least time you would take for this would be two weeks and you would spread the 35 hours out over eleven or twelve days. My recommended two-week timetable would look like this, because keeping the hours in this configuration means you are finishing each unit of work in one sitting:

PHASE 1

Sunday: 4 hours
Monday: 2 hours
Tuesday: 4 hours
Wednesday: 3 hours
Thursday: off

PHASE 2

Friday: 0–3 hours
Saturday: 1–4 hours

Sunday: 3 hours
Monday: 2 hours
Tuesday: off
Wednesday: 3 hours

PHASE 3

Thursday: 2 hours
Friday: 2 hours
Saturday/Sunday: 2 hours

Of course, there are many other ways to divide up your time. I've learned that taking days off can actually be helpful for me, so my ideal timetable includes those. You might not find it so – especially if you are feeling the pressure of time. If you work each day you can complete the full working plan in twelve days – and if you increase some of the 2-hour work slots to 4 hours, you'll finish that much faster.

For many reasons, however, the twelve-day plan is ideal, as it gives your brain a lot of reflective time in between sessions and that helps to cement the learning.

If you are doing a second monologue, you will, of course, only be doing Phases 2 and 3, but I would still recommend following the above timetable for those phases, if you can. Allowing time for your unconscious mind to work is really important and you can't do that if you are doing too many hours/days in a row.

However you divide your time, though, you need to be aware of taking things in bite-sized chunks. This is because for most people, our ability to stay focused on a task begins to decline after about 20 minutes. You can increase this if you are really interested in what you are working on and some people have the ability to stay concentrated for hours. It is probably best that you set your own routine – taking breaks whenever you find yourself becoming distracted.

Don't be tempted to ignore the short breaks written into the timed working sections. They are designed to encourage your 'slow-thinking' brain to be part of the preparation process. Remember that the way you take that break is particularly important. Do not jump online or talk on the phone – those activities require focused thinking. In the break times, you want to let your mind wander. So, go outside if you can and take a short walk. Or lean back, close your eyes and just concentrate on your breathing. Perhaps you want to get up and move around. In fact, almost anything that you can do that engages you physically, rather than mentally, has been proved to be of real benefit to study.

You are going to be looking up any word in your monologue that you don't understand and you'll also want to look up some words in the exercises you find throughout the book. The best source for doing that online is: www.shakespeareswords.com. You'll find more information about this site in the Resources section.

NEVER BEGIN WORK ON A TEXT UNTIL YOU UNDERSTAND ALL OF THE WORDS. Remember that sometimes even when we know the words, we won't be entirely sure of the meaning, so at the very least do know what the words themselves mean.

Downloading and using a speech analyzer

We are going to be using technology to help us monitor our own sound. Throughout the work presented here, you'll to need to make some relatively objective judgements about the sounds you make, but this is hard to do by yourself. Because you are so accustomed to your own sound, it is difficult to achieve that level of objectivity. I think the best way to solve this problem is by downloading a piece of software that will allow you to 'see' your sound as you make it.

A speech analyzer is incredibly helpful because it provides a feedback method that isn't wholly reliant on what you hear. I am not suggesting that some mechanical feedback, like a speech analyzer, is going to help you create rich, resonant and artistically well-judged choices – those things take years of training and practice and we are working in a time-sensitive way. But an analyzer will give you quick visual feedback on the kind of sound you are making now and is also an effective way to push yourself into making bolder choices about the kinds of sounds you *COULD* be making.

No matter how many times I encourage actors to be bolder with their sounds, the fear of making big bold sounds is strong. At least with an analyzer you will have to see, rather than hear, what you are doing and that visual feedback can help you see patterns and habits in your speech that just listening to yourself won't. For example, I've often worked with actors who can't hear that they're dropping the end of every line, so it helps those actors to be able to SEE this pattern and to have a visual way of responding. Locating and downloading software shouldn't take more than 5–10 minutes. You'll find a list of suggested software in the Resources section on page 215 of the appendix. Spend time now locating and downloading a programme. Once you've done that, check your time – if all has gone well, spend any time left out the 2 hours allocated for this session to play with and get to know how the analyzer works. Experiment with it to make sure you are comfortable with recording and seeing a visual response to the sounds you can make. You don't need a lot of technical knowledge to simply notice that when you speak with a lot of vocal energy (say, a level 8 out of 10), the charts show much more variation and width. When you speak in a quiet monotone (perhaps a level 1 out of 10), the charts are very narrow and repetitive.

Here's are samples of my voice in the '1', '5' and '10' effort level ranges using the WASP analyzer:

Level 1:

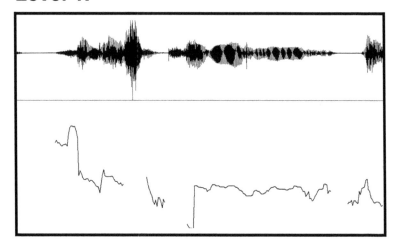

Level 5:

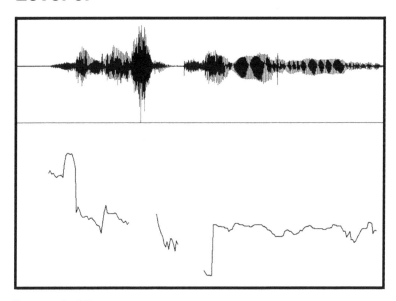

Level 10:

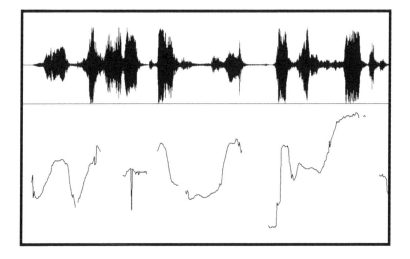

The upper graph is waveform and it is recording time and intensity. The lower graph is a pitch indicator. As you can see, the level 1 and 5 waveforms are a bit fuzzy and almost equally narrow, although the '5' has a little more muscle in it as it goes along. In levels 1 and 5, you can very clearly see that I have a habit of dropping inflection as the line goes on. The level 10 shows much greater width of intensity and I am clearly better at holding the energy and pitch of the line right the way through to the end.

I pay a lot of attention to that lower pitch graph – it shows exactly what you are doing with range as you speak and most of us need to do much more work with the range of sounds we make when speaking. That can often feel strange when we are just listening to our sound, but it becomes an interesting challenge when we are looking at sound as we make it.

Get to know, roughly, what your '1', '5' and '10' graphs look like. It is going to be very helpful to you as we go along.

PHASE 1

ACQUIRING THE SKILLS

Adding vocal colour

2 HOURS

Imagine seeing many art exhibitions in a row, all of them in black, white and grey. Imagine that wherever you went – from national galleries to fine art supply stores – you could only find black, white and grey. If you truly *could* imagine that, then you can probably roughly imagine what I go through when I serve as an audition panellist. I'm not talking here about what I see, but about what I hear. Because what I hear is mostly a *very* limited 'black-white-grey' palette of sound. Occasionally, I get a glimpse of something colourful, but rarely do I see the full spectrum of colour, weight, texture or sustained effort that one might desire in a work of art.

Before all else, we are going to look at one of the most important tools you can acquire: enhanced vocal expression. Of course, most training conservatoires spend many hours a week over two or three years to train actors' voices and we can't do that here. It is important to note that we are going to be working with the voice you have. We won't be able to go into things like resonance, placement, dialect, or even overall quality of sound. Your voice may or may not need that kind of work, but whatever point you are at in terms of training or speech quality, all we can do here is work on extending and enhancing the sound you have now in the service of expressing heightened language.

It is hard to explore new vocal possibilities if we bring our usual habits to a text. One of the things we bring is our desire to make sense (logical or emotional sense) of things as we read. If we explore in a kind of detached way, however, we tend not to worry about whether a sound 'matches' meaning, or whether a sound is the logical way to express a particular idea, or even whether we are comfortable with a sound. This is why it is so important to keep our early explorations here detached from any sense, emotion or meaning that we generate.

This doesn't mean that we won't allow what we hear or feel as a result of making sound to resonate with us somehow. But the important word in that sentence is the verb: ALLOW. Allow sound to affect you, but don't generate any meaning of your own while we do our technical work, just listen to the sound as you are making it and let it resonate with you. Enjoy the feeling of making big or unusual sounds. Subconscious responses can sometimes be valuable – let whatever comes through just come through! In the exercises that follow, we are going to find out if we can work from the 'outside-in', to push our sound palette into new areas.

Doing vocal exercises out of a book can be very difficult. I've tried to make these as simple as possible and if you do them with a speech analyzer, you should be able to see immediately if you are getting results.

Diction

Most actors understand the idea of good diction, which I'm going to refer to here as an important part of true clarity in spoken language. Of course, diction isn't the only ingredient in clear language – a slightly slower speech rate, enhanced vowel duration, expanded pitch range and greater sound pressure levels are all part of the adjustments speakers make when they're attempting to be as clear as they can be. Diction is often about creating a marked distinction in consonant sounds. We are going to concentrate on the consonants first.

Often actors find that the effort needed to produce strong, distinct consonant sounds feels rather 'fake' to them. There's only one way to get over this: familiarity. You need to get so used to expending more effort in your diction that it DOESN'T feel fake. If 90 per cent of your acting expression is carried through the medium of soft/slightly slurred consonants, whispery moments of intensity and a 'normal' speaking range, then suddenly acquiring sharp, clear consonants and as wide a vocal range as possible is going to be difficult to marry up with what you perceive to be your 'truthful' acting intentions. However, we are not going to worry about that now, because to start with, we are not going to be acting!

In Phases 1 and 2, we are going to be working in the same way that ballet dancers work at a barre or the way that piano players work on scales: that is to say, you will never see this work on stage in performance, but barre exercises and piano scales are the building blocks of great performance for both artists. Great diction, resonant and clear sound and impressive vocal range are some of the key building blocks for a great performance when it comes to text this rich. Don't be tempted to skip any of these sections – the timed exercises are all part of the 35 hours that we know we'll need in order to feel confident as we walk through those audition doors.

Sound has an emotional effect. Even sound devoid of all feeling or thought can inspire an emotional response from us. In all the exercises that follow, we are going to begin with the experience of sound and simply see how sound resonates within us, and how it may inspire thought or feeling. You won't need anything but concentration in order to do this.

EXERCISE 1: CONSONANT EFFORT

Imagine a scale of sound that you can make with a consonant, from very, very soft to very, very hard and almost popping. We are going to begin by working at the extreme ends of the consonant sound that you can make. Speak these sentences out loud, starting with the softest consonant sounds you can make. This is simple in the case of soft consonants like S, F or V, but more challenging with hard or plosive consonants like P, B, or D.

Watch your sound on a speech analyzer – first with the very softest possible consonant sounds you can make, perhaps what might be a 1 on a scale of 1 to 10. Then speak them through neutrally, or what might be a 5 on a scale of 1 to 10. Next, speak them with the strongest, crispest, most popping diction you can manage – as close as you can get to a 10 on the scale of 1 to 10. On the analyzer, you are going for the greatest range of graph usage that you can.

As you do this, simply notice what feels different as you go from 1 to 5 to 10. Most people find that softening consonants down to a '1' level is difficult, so you'll want to practice these. The level '10' sounds can be challenging to sustain all the way through a sentence, so keep your concentration there as well. Allow yourself to reflect on what kind of feeling or thoughts seem to accompany the sounds as you make them. You'll probably notice nothing when you speak at the neutral level. But there may be things that you feel or think as you speak at the 1 or the 10 level.

1   I particularly begged him not to pester you like that.
2   For heaven's sake, how could she make that kind of inconsiderate decision?
3   Don't rush into taking the flat before we've talked.
4   Make one more move, mister, and make it count.
5   Let me be very clear: the time to think about it is over
6   Just go now – go! Not tomorrow, now!
7   Ring him? Don't you think I've tried to ring him?
8   Take ten seconds to think about it before tossing everything away.
9   Very funny – very appropriate. Now you know why I'm over him.
10 What would make you want to live in this filth?

These first sentences are typical of contemporary theatre texts, so the diction might feel most 'natural' to you as an actor at the '5' level.

   Now do the same exercise with these sentences from Shakespeare, going through once at level 1, once at level 5, and once at level 10. Use the analyzer again:

1   Be absolute for death.
2   Your grace shall pardon me, I will not back.
3   But God, he knows, thy share thereof is small
4   Ambitious York doth level at thy crown
5   O Tiger's heart wrapped in a woman's hide!
6   What, my dear lady disdain! Are you yet living?
7   I would rather hear my dog bark at a crow than
    A man swear he loves me.
8   Dishonour not her honourable name,
    To make a bastard and a slave of me!
9   How oft the sight of means to do ill deeds
    Make deeds ill done!
10 A heavier task could not have been imposed
    Than I to speak my griefs unspeakable

It is likely that the level '10' effort on consonants here felt much more comfortable on this second set of lines than it did on the first. That's only because you are used to hearing and speaking lines that are like the contemporary sentences we did before and you don't ordinarily hear or speak in the language of the second set of lines. For that reason, more effort and more 'poppingly' clean diction might have felt powerful rather than fake. This may seem obvious but it is no small point when we are trying to gear up for a great performance in heightened text. And, while this exercise isn't greatly challenging, it does require that you spend a little time with it and get to feel what 'level 10' type consonants do for diction. What you need to remember is that if level '5' feels ordinary or neutral to you, then you will always be aiming for at least a level 7 consonant sound when you are working with Shakespeare.

Do this exercise enough times to be able to distinguish for yourself what a level '7' effort feels like: it won't be as outrageous or as strenuous as your level '10', but it won't be as easy as your neutral '5' effort. This is a critical piece of self-monitoring in your preparation. Stay with this exercise until you are confident that you can feel the difference between a level 5, a level 10 and a level 7 effort.

The final part of this exercise is to go back to the set of Shakespeare sentences above and do them again at level 10. It is very likely that your first attempts at level 10 consonant effort made the lines all sound the same: it may have made all of them sound angry or cynical. This time, go through the sentences and see if you can hang on to your level 10 of consonant effort but this time, try consciously varying both the pitch and speed at which you speak. Practice this until you can get through all 10 without sounding angry all the time. Watch the pitch graph in your analyzer and make it as wide as you can. Wide variations of pitch along with popping consonants can give the sentences a very different effect.

It is important to get used to practicing at level 10, for the same reason that some athletes work with weights on their ankles – once the weights are gone the athlete's legs feel light and nimble. So it is with speech practice – the longer you remain at level 10, the lighter and more nimble you'll sound at level 7 – which is what you are generally aiming for in performance.

Sustaining sound

We are very used to the concept of vocal sustain in singers. Along with wide variation in pitch and melody, it is what distinguishes singing from speaking. But we can be very uncomfortable with sustain in speaking. That's because in ordinary speech, we don't tend to sustain much when we are talking and indeed, we speak at a pretty rapid pace in our day-to-day exchanges. But our day-to-day speech is readily understood by those around us and it is rare that we break into language that requires a bit more time and effort for our audience to take in.

Of course, Shakespeare's language DOES take that bit more time and effort from our audience and that's one reason that exploiting sustain a bit in our speech when performing can help with clarity. But there's another great reason for sustaining sound when working on Shakespeare, and that is just the simple beauty of so much of his language.

The great majority of contemporary realism that you will work on as an actor doesn't focus terribly much on the beauty of the language. Writers like Harold Pinter, Caryl Churchill or David Mamet sometimes produce scripts in which language is reduced to a minimum; where three- or four-word sentences, followed by a mysterious … ellipsis can be the norm.

These writers have brilliant ways of capturing the uncertain rhythms and the incomplete thoughts behind real conversation, and their dialogue can feel so natural. No doubt it is just his brilliance in capturing natural conversational rhythms that inspired Mamet to write to actors that they didn't need to do anything other than speak his lines. Everything else would be done for them by the text. As you work with contemporary writers it is rarely the language itself that you focus on – instead, the beauty of many contemporary scripts lies elsewhere: in the atmosphere, the characters, the wit, or the tensions the writer creates. When you are working with scripts like these, your focus is on getting right inside the sense of what you want, how you are going to manipulate those around into doing what you want, and on how securely you can imagine the world of the play.

Shakespeare's texts require those things, too, but they require much more in a technical sense. They require that you are able to make some very tough language very clear to an audience. And that means sometimes you want to linger over sound a bit. That can be simply because you love the effect your sound is having on the person you are speaking to. It can be because you want to make the pleasure of your words last longer. It can be because the words are so powerful that you are reluctant to let them go. Whatever the reason, a little more sustain, or vowel extension, not only allows you to enjoy what you are doing, it gives your audience a little time to catch up with what you are saying.

We can't sustain every sound, although we can always sustain vowel sounds. Consonants can be trickier, as you'll discover once we start trying them. The harder, plosive consonants (P, T, D, B, K, G) don't work with sustain at all. Some of the softer, fricative consonants (F, V, Th, Sh, S, Z) sustain well. Sounds like Ch, R, and soft G (as in gem) can be sustained too, but might not sound quite as easy. Still, the best way to learn is to try!

With this next exercise we are simply going to do this rather mechanically at first. Because sustaining sound is so foreign to us in our conversational speech mode, we just have to MAKE ourselves make these sounds often enough that we will come to feel more at ease when we decide to use them in our performance.

EXERCISE 2: SOUND EXTENSION

Speak these sentences out loud and speech analyze as you do. Do these at least twice. Allow as much sustain as you can (and for as long as you can), while still keeping the meaning of the sentence. It is a bit of a challenge in some of them, but, with a little practice, you should be able to manage it. It will help if you try these out first and circle the vowels/ consonants that you feel you can comfortably sustain while keeping some meaning in the sound of the sentence:

1 Oh yes, do give me that.
2 Why did you have to say tonight?
3 Now that I have your attention: please don't do it.
4 Go, now, just leave off talking about your so-called life and go.
5 No please, listen, you've got to make her hear reason.
6 Smooth and luscious – I told you homemade ice cream was great.

7   Oh, leave those things on the chair and come sit with me on the floor.

8   You wanted all this for yourself; you never thought of me.

9   Here you go: every last, leftover, sentimental card.

10   In this instance, it would be so much more appreciated if you could.

This exercise can sometimes make people feel as if they're whining. So, just as you did with the first exercise (where diction effort can sometimes make everything sound angry), go back and repeat the exercise, and this time try to keep your sustain, and keep the sense of the words, but try varying pitch and upping consonant effort to see if you can keep the sentences from all sounding the same. Do these exercises with no emotional content – just linger where you feel you can, and see how the sound affects you, and think a bit about how the lingering sound affects the meaning of the words.

For most actors, lingering or sustaining feels much more 'fake' than even level 10 effort on diction. This is because our natural speaking speed is so fast. But this exercise is even more like the athlete who works with weights on so that once released, they feel light and nimble. Sustain is a kind of weight that you have to practice with. The idea is not so much that you will speak this way when performing – but the occasional sustain is a great way to emphasize an important action in a speech and is seldom used by actors, despite its power.

Sustain also usually makes an actor explore range a bit more, since it can be quite dull and inexpressive to sustain for long on one spoken pitch. For this reason alone it is an important exercise. Use a speech analyzer, and try to get the widest readings possible in the 'pitch' graph when you are doing these sustains.

Forcing ourselves to sustain also makes us aware of the sound of the language and the kind of power we have through sustain. Hanging onto it in performance – especially audition performance – is a very difficult thing to do, given that audition nerves often speed us up. That's another reason why exercising sustain is so important at this stage.

SUMMARY EXERCISES

*We are going to practice sustained sound again, only this time we are
going to add some crisp consonants in any place that we feel would
make the meaning of the words clearer. Sustain or use 'popping'
consonants just because of the beauty or the uniqueness of the sound.
Go through the Shakespeare phrases and sentences below at least
twice, and sustain the vowel sounds or pop the consonants in the words
you like best, while still keeping the meaning of the sentence. Again, use
speech analyzer on all of these summary exercises.*

1 Ope not thy ponderous and marble jaws.
2 Thou art death's fool, for him thou labourest
3 A heavy heart hears not a nimble tongue
4 How slow this old moon wanes! She lingers my desires.
5 Duller shoulds't thou be than the fat weed.
6 I am a scribbled form, drawn with a pen upon a parchment.
7 Are you a god? Would you create me new?
    Transform me then and to your power I'll yield.
8 And when love speaks, the voice of all the gods
    Make heaven drowsy with the harmony
9 Oh for a muse of fire, that would ascend the brightest heaven of
    invention.
10 What plain proceeding is more plain than this? Henry doth claim the
    crown from John of Gaunt.

On this final set of sentences, aim to stay between a level 5 and level 8.
Have a look at your speech analyzer graphs, as they should be a good
visual guide to distinguishing between a level 5 and a level 8. Go through
each sentence three times and, each time, try to vary your vocal pitch,
pop some of your consonants and work on vowel duration:

1 My Lord I do desire you do me right and justice.
2 But what of that? Demetrius thinks not so.
3 Therefore this maxim out of love I teach

4   Achievement is command, ungained beseech.
5   Oh what a rogue and peasant slave am I
6   Now is the winter of our discontent
7   Made glorious summer by this son of York.
8   And fill me from the crown to the toe top-full
9   Of direst cruelty! Make thick my blood;
10 Methinks I hear him now; his plausive words

In this final practice, read the Shakespeare lines once, then the modern equivalents. Use speech analyzer on each. Aim for a '5' effort level on the modern equivalent and, using heightened diction and sustain, aim for a '7' or higher effort level on the Shakespeare lines. As ever, don't worry about 'acting' or getting emotion involved – concentrate on sound.

Shakespeare	Modern equivalent
Then let the earth be drunken with our blood	Then let's have a bloody fight
Smile gentle heaven, or strike, ungentle death; For this world frowns and Edward's sun is clouded.	Let me live or let me die, Since nothing is going well for Edward.
Oh Goneril, You are not worth the dust which the rude wind blows in your face	Oh Goneril, You are worthless
'Tis strange that death should sing. I am the cygnet to this pale faint swan Who chants a doleful hymn to his own death.	How weird that death seems musical. I'm like a child, singing my own death song.
I am a scribbled form, drawn with a pen Upon a parchment, and against this fire Do I shrink up.	I'm hot and dry and I seem to be near death.
Will Fortune never come with both hands full But write her fair words still in foulest letters?	Although the news is good, I'm worried other bad things will happen.

Shakespeare	Modern equivalent
For treason is but trusted like the fox who, ne'er so tame, so cherish'd and lock'd up Will have a wild trick of his ancestors	Once we've been traitors, no one will ever trust us again. No matter how honest we look, we'll always be traitors.
Let them come! They come like sacrifices in their trim and to the Fire-eye'd maid of smokey war All hot and bleeding will we offer them	Bring them on! They're going to die in a bloody battle, and we'll sacrifice them to the god of war.
Cry Havoc! And let slip the dogs of war.	Shout and declare war!
I do love nothing in the world so well as you. Is not that strange?	I love you more than anything. Isn't that odd?

I'm hoping this summary exercise will achieve two things:

1   it should heighten your awareness of how various techniques work in making the Shakespeare text come alive, and

2   it should make clear why Shakespeare's language (when compared to its contemporary counterpart) is such a treat for actors to speak.

Check your time now and if there's any left of your two hours, keep working on the exercises.

What's the point of mastering meter?

2 HOURS

We've gone through the fundamental sound tools we need for our work and we now need to acquire two analytical tools. The first will help you to get over your fear of speaking and working in verse. Because the majority of Shakespeare's work is in verse, it is statistically likely that your monologue will be in verse. If, however, you are doing a monologue in prose and you are under time stress, you can come back to this section when you have more time – for now, go straight on to the next timed section. If your monologue is in verse, though, stay with this as you'll find it incredibly helpful in terms of memorization and in gaining confidence with the verse. Before we get on to that, however, I need to make a point about stressing syllables when we speak.

The whole idea of verse meter is based on the idea of stressing one syllable over the other. Even the simplest nursery rhyme works on this basic principle. The fact is that we naturally select stress in speech all the time – and that stress, which we create either through enhanced volume or range or syllable duration, is important in terms of listener comprehension. This is a simple enough idea to illustrate in one word: present. We know that if we stress the first syllable PRE-, the listener will know that you are either talking about a gift (a birthday present) or about someone or something being in a particular place (he was present). But if you stress the second syllable, -SENT, the listener will know that you meant showing or giving something (she had to present a paper).

We have to remember that while there are stress rules, the rules change in varying contexts. I find this to be true when I look at Shakespeare's texts. It may be that the stress suggested by his meter feels right. It may be that it feels wrong. But EVERYTHING depends on the context in which it is found.

Looking at rhythm

There's a lot of anxiety about verse speaking and how to do it 'right'. I think there are also a number of views on the whole point of looking at verse structure – and certainly not everyone agrees on just how important it may be in performance. But everyone agrees on one thing: observing the meter SHOULDN'T trap you into sounding repetitive or 'sing-songy'.

After many years of working on Shakespeare, I've come to believe that there are only FOUR irrefutable reasons for actors to spend time looking at the verse structure in a text they're working on:

1   It will help you figure out how a line should sound – not in terms of your own interpretive reading, but in terms of pronunciation, and overall preparation of the text for performing (elisions, 'soft' stresses, etc.).

2   It can sometimes give you some good ideas for your reading of a line in performance and/or some unexpected and brilliant ways to read a scene.

3   It will definitely help your memorization of text.

4   It will help you to maintain a strength and muscularity through a line that helps the listener.

I'm going to focus on the things I think are most important when you are first approaching an audition monologue in verse, and I know that there are many fine points and details about verse and verse structure that we won't get to here, since we are in a time-critical situation. But as we are working on meter, we need to keep in mind the four ideas above, in the hope that you will begin to see the significant help that verse analysis can give you. To get started, this section is going to look specifically at how iambic pentameter sounds. And in order to do that we are going to start by considering how it LOOKS.

I think a visual approach is the clearest for understanding the structure of iambic pentameter verse when you are just getting started. So, we are going to 'look' at the verse as well as listen to it. In this visual representation, every BOLD CAPITAL SYLLABLE is a stressed syllable and a lower-case syllable is not. As you go through this section,

<u>read every line out loud and in meter</u>. We start with an even iambic pentameter line, which looks like this:

ta-**DUM** ta-**DUM** ta-**DUM** ta-**DUM** ta-**DUM**

As simple as this seems, I've seen people struggle with it, so before we go on, go over that line above and do it until the rhythm of it feels absolutely, rhythmically solid to you. If it is hard for you to feel when reading out loud, try walking in time with the rhythm and stomping very hard on a stressed syllable.

When you've got that, then we are going to try that sound out loud on two perfectly even lines:

In sooth, I know not why I am so sad
It wearies me, you say it wearies you.

If we 'look' at them in meter, they look like this:

In **SOOTH**, I **KNOW** not **WHY** I **AM** so **SAD**
It **WEAR** ies **ME**, you **SAY** it **WEAR** ies **YOU**

If you've covered this before and this comes easily to your ear, just read the lines above out loud and then move on. If this is all new for you, read the lines above enough times that you can feel the rhythm of the iambic pentameter quite solidly.

EXERCISE 1: EVEN METER LINES

What makes a line even is not simply that it falls into the rhythm neatly; it is also that the words SOUND right in the rhythm. Just to cement that sound in your head and heart, read the following even lines out loud at least three times, exaggerating the meter stress. For this exercise, you want your reading to sound almost 'sing-songy' as you go through, so that you are getting used to the sound of the rhythm. It is important in this process to resist your desire to 'act' – leave all of that to one side and just let the sound and rhythm emerge. Listen, remember anything that you like the sound of, remember anything that resonates with you, but apart from making the rhythm very obvious as you speak it, don't do anything more than that.

Your grace shall pardon me I will not back

Your **GRACE** shall **PAR** don **ME**, I **WILL** not **BACK**

There is no reason but I shall be blind

There **IS** no **REA** son **BUT** I **SHALL** be **BLIND**

I, by the honour of my marriage bed

I, **BY** the **HON** our **OF** my **MAR** riage **BED**

If I can check my erring love I will

If **I** can **CHECK** my **ERR** ing **LOVE** I **WILL**

He will suspect us still and find a time

He **WILL** sus **PECT** us **STILL** and **FIND** a **TIME**

You have some sick offence within your mind

You **HAVE** some **SICK** of **FENCE** with **IN** your **MIND**

Or fill up chronicles in time to come

Or **FILL** up **CHRON** i **CLES** in **TIME** to **COME**

Shall it for shame be spoken in these days

Shall **IT** for **SHAME** be **SPO** ken **IN** these **DAYS**

O, pardon me that I descend so low

O, **PAR** don **ME** that **I** des **CEND** so **LOW**

If not, to compass her I'll use my skill

If **NOT**, to **COM** pass **HER** I'll **USE** my **SKILL**

Good pilgrim you do wrong your hand too much

Good **PIL** grim **YOU** do **WRONG** your **HAND** too **MUCH**

I wonder how the king escaped our hands

I **WON** der **HOW** the **KING** es **CAPED** our **HANDS**

Yet more in Troilus thousand-fold I see

Yet **MORE** in **TROI** lus **THOU** sand- **FOLD** I **SEE**

Oh, time thou must untangle this, not I

Oh, **TIME** thou **MUST** un **TAN** gle **THIS,** not **I**

What was it you that would be England's king?

What **WAS** it **YOU** that **WOULD** be **ENG** land's **KING**?

But soft, what light from yonder window shines?

But **SOFT**, what **LIGHT** from **YON** der **WIN** dow **SHINES**?

There let him sink and be the seas on him

There **LET** him **SINK** and **BE** the **SEAS** on **HIM**

Put on what weary negligence you please

Put **ON** what **WEA** ry **NEG** li **GENCE** you **PLEASE**

But screw your courage to the sticking place

But **SCREW** your **COU** rage **TO** the **STIC** king **PLACE**

Oh what a rogue and peasant slave am I

Oh **WHAT** a **ROGUE** and **PEA** sant **SLAVE** am **I**

'Feminine' endings

A 'feminine' line has one extra syllable and sounds like this:

ta- **DUM** ta- **DUM** ta- **DUM** ta- **DUM** ta- **DUM** ta

Here are two lines with 'feminine' endings:

To be or not to be, that is the question
With that same purpose changer that sly devil

If we 'look' at them in meter, they look like this:

To **BE** or **NOT** to **BE**, that **IS** the **QUES** tion

With **THAT** same **PUR** pose **CHANG** er **THAT** sly **DEV** il

You will notice that these lines SOUND right in the rhythm, but they simply have one extra unstressed syllable. Sometimes that lack of stress sounds exactly right – the way it does with these two lines. We would very naturally stress the first syllable of both words 'question' and 'devil'. But sometimes it doesn't feel right to lose the stress on the final syllable.

EXERCISE 2: FEMININE ENDINGS

These lines might sound strange as you do them out loud, especially after the practice with the even lines. But for the most part, the lines with feminine endings sound right to our ears, even with that last unstressed extra syllable. Read all these lines out loud and, again, exaggerate the meter stresses as you go, and let the rhythm dominate.

Did ever in so true a flame of liking

Did **EV** er **IN** so **TRUE** a **FLAME** of **LIK** ing

Or as one nail by strength drives out another

Or **AS** one **NAIL** by **STRENGTH** drives **OUT** an **OTH** er

Apt, liable to be employ'd in danger

Apt, **LI** a **BLE** to **BE** em **PLOY'D** in **DANG** er

You lean'd unto his sentence with what patience

You **LEAN'D** un **TO** his **SENT** ence **WITH** what **PA** tience

A woman moved is like a fountain troubled

A **WO** man **MOVED** is **LIKE** a **FOUN** tain **TROUB** led

So thou that hast no unkind mate to grieve thee

So **THOU** that **HAST** no **UN** kind **MATE** to **GRIEVE** thee

High birth, vigour of bone, desert in service

High **BIRTH**, vig **OUR** of **BONE**, de **SERT** in **SERV** ice

Or to take arms against a sea of troubles

Or **TO** take **ARMS** a **GAINST** a **SEA** of **TROUB** les

Our house is hell, and thou, a merry devil

Our **HOUSE** is **HELL**, and **THOU**, a **MER** ry **DEV** il

What great creation and what dole of honour

What **GREAT** cre **A** tion **AND** what **DOLE** of **HON** our

We'll have a swashing and a martial outside

We'll **HAVE** a **SWASH** ing **AND** a **MAR** tial **OUT** side

Sign me a present pardon for my brother

Sign **ME** a **PRE** sent **PAR** don **FOR** my **BRO** ther

The testimony on my part no other

The **TEST** i **MO** ny **ON** my **PART** no **OTH** er

That Mowbray hath received eight thousand nobles

That **MOW** bray **HATH** re **CEIVED** eight **THOU** sand **NOB** les

My very noble and approv'd good masters

My **VE** ry **NO** ble **AND** a **PPROV'D** good **MAS** ters

Shall ever take alive the noble Brutus

Shall **E** ver **TAKE** a **LIVE** the **NO** ble **BRU** tus

He purposed to his wife's sole son—a widow

He **PUR** posed **TO** his **WIFE'S** sole **SON** – a **WID** ow

'Rocking'[1] lines

An uneven or 'rocking' line can take many forms:
    I would call these 'rocking' lines, because they don't simply have an extra syllable. They 'rock' because they just don't sound right in iambic pentameter – the stress feels as if it is in all the wrong places:

My Lord of Westmoreland lead him to his tent
Come, my lord, I'll lead you to your tent

You can hear that as you read them in meter:

My **LORD** of **WEST** more **LAND** lead **HIM** to **HIS** tent

Come, **MY** lord, **I'LL** lead **YOU** to **YOUR** tent

Verbs are vital in helping a listener make sense of Shakespeare's language. But if you look at the words that are stressed in the two lines above, you'll see that they are almost entirely pronouns. The repeated verb 'lead' is never stressed, nor is the single other verb, 'come', nor is the repeated object, 'tent'. When you read the lines as they are stressed above they sound seriously wrong! Remember that what is paramount in speaking Shakespeare's verse is to make it clear to the listener and to help the listener follow the action. When the meter doesn't help with either of these things, then it's time to stop worrying about it. Put your concentration instead on making the line as clear as it can be.

---

[1] This is Cicely Berry's term for awkward lines that do not 'speak' easily in the meter.

Some 'rocking' lines feel almost as if they're simply NOT in verse –
even when it is clear that everything around them is. This one is stuck
in the midst of a perfectly even lot of lines:

He will suspect us still and find a time
To punish this offense in other faults
Supposition all our lives shall be stuck full of eyes.
For treason is but trusted like the fox.

There is absolutely no way to scan that third line in verse. It sticks out
like a sore thumb, and perhaps the actor playing this role might want
to think about why that particular line stands out so much. Perhaps at
this point, Worcester feels the need to over-emphasise the danger of
accepting the King's offer of mercy here. Thinking about this falls into
the second point I raised above, about how looking at verse structure
and rhythm can sometimes give us ideas about how to actually play
a line. Maybe the idea of being closely watched for the rest of his life
holds a particular terror for Worcester? Perhaps the actor playing this
role will find it worthwhile to contemplate why this line stands out on
its own. Shakespeare often allowed important lines to stand out in this
way, and this is one of the ways in which analysing the verse can help
us to understand the language.

When to contract and when to expand

Elisions

We can use meter to help us prepare a text for performance. Probably
the most important way it does that is to reveal where to use elision
and where to pronounce the final '-ed' of a word. Elisions are simply
the dropping of a letter to shorten a word.

These can be tricky and the only way to learn is to trust your ear.
That's why it is important to do all these exercises out loud – it is a way
of training your ear.

Sometimes Shakespeare does the elisions for you, and whenever
you are pronouncing an elision, you pronounce the consonants and
vowels in exactly the same way that you would if the dropped letter
was still there:

England ne'er had a king until his time *('never' has become one syllable)*

> Eng **LAND** ne'er **HAD** a **KING** un **TIL** his **TIME**
> ('ne'er' is pronounced like 'where')

O, no; wherein Lord Talbot was o'erthrown: *('over' has become one syllable)*

> O, **NO;** where **IN** Lord **TAL** bot **WAS** o'er **THROWN**
> ('o'er' should rhyme with 'for')

Bright star of Venus, fall'n down on the earth *('fallen' has become one syllable)*

> Bright **STAR** of **VE** nus, **FALL'N** down **ON** the **EARTH**
> ('fall'n' should sound like 'qualm')

Faint-hearted Woodvile, prizest him 'fore me? (*'afore' or 'before' has become one syllable*)

> Faint- **HEAR** ted **WOOD** vile, **PRIZ** est **HIM** 'fore **ME**

As you can see, all the elisions that Shakespeare himself has done were done to transform an uneven line into an even one. Make sure you never add the dropped syllable back in. Perhaps nothing marks the novice Shakespearean more than an actor who corrects his elisions. 'Had'st' or 'Would'st' are always one syllable – never add one back ('Had-est' or 'Would-est')!

There are times, however, when these are not done for you and sometimes this can be a tricky matter – more of an art than a science, certainly.

Sometimes a feminine line can sound almost even if the last syllable is very soft. Look at this line from King John:

With that same purpose-changer, that sly devil

> With **THAT** same **PUR** pose- **CHAN** ger, **THAT** sly **DEV'L**

The last syllable of 'devil' is so soft, it almost sounds like a single syllable anyway, so your natural reading of it might almost sound like an elision.

But what about lines where that isn't true? Read this line out:

The insulting hand of Douglas over you

The **IN** sult **ING** hand **OF** Doug **LAS** o **VER** you

When read in meter the line sounds quite awkward, because all the stresses are in the wrong place. But if we elide the opening 'the', making 'th'in' one syllable, we can make the entire line even and it will sound better:

Th'in **SULT** ing **HAND** of **DOUG** las **O** ver **YOU**

The same is true of this line, which sounds all wrong if stressed as a regular feminine line:

Being men of such great leading as you are

Be **ING** men **OF** such **GREAT** lead **ING** as **YOU** are

But once again, we can elide the two-syllable 'being' as one syllable: 'b'ing', and create an even line that sounds exactly right:

B'ing **MEN** of **SUCH** great **LEAD** ing **AS** you **ARE**

Now the line sounds strong and sensible in meter.

Added syllables

Sometimes the text requires that we do the opposite; sometimes we need ADDED SYLLABLES make an uneven line even. For example:

Enlarged him and made a friend of him

En **LARGED** him **AND** made **A** friend **OF** him

If stressed the way it is above, it sounds as if the line is short – it seems to have one syllable less than it needs. It also sounds very awkward in meter because it stresses all the unimportant words. But if we add a syllable to 'enlarged' it all comes right:

En **LARG** ed **HIM** and **MADE** a **FRIEND** of **HIM**

The same is true of this line:

Myself condemned and myself excused

Which sounds both short and strange if we don't add a stress to ONE of the '-ed' suffixes:

My **SELF** con **DEMNED** and **MY** self **EX** cused

Now this is a tricky one, because we could add a stress to the final '-ed':

My **SELF** con **DEMNED** and **MY** self **EX** cus **ED**

But to my ear, this still puts stress in the wrong places (my, ex). But if I add the extra '-ed' to 'condemned' instead, it all sounds better:

My **SELF** con **DEM** ned **AND** my **SELF** ex **CUSED**

Take a moment and look back at that line now, because it demonstrates the way in which analyzing verse can tell you so much about what the line actually means. Ordinarily, we wouldn't particularly want to stress a word like AND, the way we do above. But in this case, the Friar is talking to Romeo about the fact that by helping him and Juliet, he sees that he is doing both right **AND** wrong. And so it is that he stands both condemned AND excused – therefore the 'and' is vital.

Eliding and expanding at the same time

And just to add one final complication – sometimes we do **BOTH** to make a line sound better. Take this line from King John:

Their battering cannon charged to the mouths

Their **BAT** ter **ING** can **NON** charged **TO** the **MOUTHS**

As you can see, it is even but it doesn't sound right, because many of the stresses are in the wrong place. It helps a little to create an elision in 'battering', so that we are not stressing the 'ing':

Their **BATT** 'ring **CAN** non **CHARGED** to **THE** mouths

Of course, now the stress on THE makes the line rock and it lacks a syllable, since we elided 'batt'ring'. We can fix this, though, by adding a syllable to 'charged':

Their **BATT** 'ring **CAN** non **CHARG** ed **TO** the **MOUTHS**

And NOW the line sounds right! It is even and it makes sense as you listen to it. As complicated as that last example is, it is the perfect demonstration of why doing this careful preparation of the text helps you find the right sound when you are performing.

Meter is a one of Shakespeare's great challenges – it both enlightens and baffles us at once. Cicely Berry says that it is 'by far the most complex factor to explain'.[2] I think you need to accept that feeling comfortable with meter is something that only comes with time. We are under pressure to prepare, so we can only consider all the fine points briefly. But even a brief consideration is helpful. Make sure you don't allow yourself to get too worried about meter in your preparation. Wherever it helps your understanding, or gives you better, more interesting ways to play a line, enjoy it. Wherever it is clear, enjoy it. Where it is not, do the best you can with it, and let your heart lead the work. You have a lifetime to master it!

---

[2] *The Actor and His Text*, p. 81.

EXERCISE 3

Identify the meter in each line of these excerpts by circling the stressed syllables. If it sounds better to you to create an elision, or add an extra syllable, do so. Read each line out loud as you go, and see if the meter feels easy and natural to you. If there are places where it doesn't, try gently evening out the stress so that you aren't putting emphasis in any place that contradicts meaning or the usual sound of a word. Remember to look up any words you don't understand – use a source like www.shakespeareswords.com.

I.

I prithee when thou see'st that act afoot,
Even with the very comment of thy soul
Observe my uncle. If his occulted guilt
Do not itself unkennel in one speech
It is a damned ghost that we have seen

II.

Your wondrous rare description, noble earl,
Of beauteous Margaret hath astonished me.
Her virtues, graced with external gifts,
Do breed love's settled passions in my heart.

III.

From off the gates of York fetch down the head,
Your father's head, which Clifford placed there;
Instead whereof let this supply the room:
Measure for measure must be answered.

IV.

Now my soul's palace is become a prison:
Ah, would she break from hence, that this my body
Might in the ground be closed up in rest!
For never henceforth shall I joy again

V.

all plum'd like estridges that with the wind
Bated, like eagles, having lately bath'd
Glittering in golden coats like images
As full of spirit as the month of May

VI.

I'll make my heaven to dream upon the crown;
And, whiles I live, t'account this world but hell,
until my misshap'd trunk that bears this head
Be round impaled with a glorious crown

Take the time to work these out before you look at the possible answers, because the best way to learn is to try it for yourself.

Some possible answers for Exercise 3

I.

I prithee when thou see'st that act afoot,
> *(no action needed – this is an even line)*

Even with the very comment of thy soul
> *(elide 'Even': E'en **WITH** the **VE** ry **COM** ment **OF** thy **SOUL**)*

Observe my uncle. If his occulted guilt
> *(because there is a full stop in the middle of the line, you can just accept this as a full break in the meter, and keep the meter even on both sides of the full stop)*

Do not itself unkennel in one speech
> *(no action needed – this is an even line)*

It is a damned ghost that we have seen
> *(sound the '–ed' of 'damned' to add a syllable and make the line even: It **IS** a **DAM** ned **GHOST** that **WE** have **SEEN**)*

II.

Your wondrous rare description, noble earl,
> *(no action needed – this is an even line)*

Of beauteous Margaret hath astonished me.
> *(elide 'beauteous' & 'Margaret': of **BEAUT** e'us **MAR** g'ret **HATH** a **STON** ished **ME**)*

Her virtues, graced with external gifts
> *(sound the '-ed of 'graced' to add a syllable and make the line even: Her* **VIR** *tues,* **GRA** *ced* **WITH** *ex* **TER** *nal* **GIFTS)**

Do breed love's settled passions in my heart.
> *(no action needed – this is an even line)*

III.

From off the gates of York fetch down the head,
> *(no action needed – this is an even line)*
> *Your father's head, which Clifford placed there;*
> *(sound the '-ed of 'placed' to add a syllable and make the line even:* *Your* **FA** *thers* **HEAD** *, which* **CLIF** *ford* **PLA** *ced* **THERE)**

Instead whereof let this supply the room:
> *(no action needed – this is an even line)*

Measure for measure must be answered.
> *(sound the '-ed' of 'answered' to add a syllable and make the line even.* *The first 2 syllables of this line are reversed, so place the stress on the* *first syllable and keep the rest in meter:* **MEAS** *ure for* **MEAS** *ure* **MUST** *be* **AN** *swer* **ED)**

IV.

Now my soul's palace is become a prison:
> *(no action needed – this is an otherwise even feminine line)*

Ah, would she break from hence, that this my body
> *(no action needed – this is an otherwise even feminine line)*

Might in the ground be closed up in rest!
> *(Sound the '-ed' of 'closed' to add a syllable and make the line even:* *might* **IN** *the* **GROUND** *be* **CLO** *sed* **UP** *in* **REST)**

For never henceforth shall I joy again
> *(no action needed – this is an even line)*

V.

all plum'd like estridges that with the wind
> *(no action needed – this is an even line)*

Bated, like eagles, having lately bath'd
> *(no action needed – this is an even line, but 'ba TED' sound rocky, so* *keep the first two syllables equal: bat ed like* **EA** *gles* **HAV** *in* **LATE** *ly* **BATH'D)**

Glittering in golden coats like images
> *(elide 'glittering': glit* **'RING** *in* **GOLD** *en* **COATS** *like* **IM** *a* **GES)**

As full of spirit as the month of May
> *(no action needed – this is an even line)*

VI.
I'll make my heaven to dream upon the crown;
> *(elide 'heaven': I'll* **MAKE** *my* **HEAV'N** *to* **DREAM** *up* **ON** *the* **CROWN***)*

And, whiles I live, t'account this world but hell,
> *(no action needed – this is an even line)*

Until my misshap'd trunk that bears this head
> *(no action needed – this is an even line)*

Be round impaled with a glorious crown
> *(sound the '-ed' of 'impaled' to add a syllable and elide 'glorious' to two syllables to make the line even: Be* **ROUND** *im* **PAL** *ed* **WITH** *a* **GLOR** *i'us* **CROWN***)*

The value of iambic pentameter

It may well be that even after observing the verse pattern and working it through with a particular text, you are still worried about it. And it makes sense that you would be. What most actors worry about first is that if you observe it too closely you'll be trapped in that rhythm and sound 'sing-songy' or artificial.

Most seasoned Shakespeare actors, directors or vocal coaches will swear that the 'pulse' of the meter gives the line life and that the more you observe it, the less artificial, in fact, you'll sound. But I've learned that this view certainty isn't universally shared. As an actor you'll ultimately make your own decisions about just how you want to observe the pulse of the meter when you are performing, but the more you observe it in your early stages of learning a text, the more you will grow to like the sound as you deepen your thought processes in rehearsal.

What is certain is that working with the pulse of the meter early on will absolutely achieve three things for you:

1   It will greatly aid your memorization. Rhythm is always a good mnemonic device and working through the rhythm in your early stages of rehearsal will help you remember all the words.

2   It will lead you make some interesting discoveries about

choices and actions that you may never have thought of before listening to the rhythm of the text.

3   It will help you retain the strength and sound of a line in a way that makes it much clearer for a listening audience.

SUMMARY EXERCISE

Read through all the lines in Exercise 3, using a speech analyzer. Read first in your own natural speech pattern and then read with a very strong emphasis on the meter. Compare the way your two readings look on the analyzer.

Here are my samples – the first is just my own natural speech pattern on a line, and as you see there are two places of strong stress and the rest is pretty undistinguished:

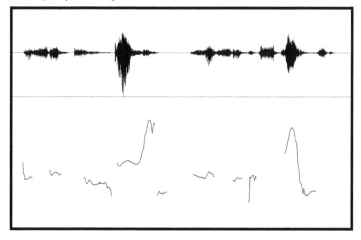

Here is a graph with me emphasizing the meter quite powerfully:

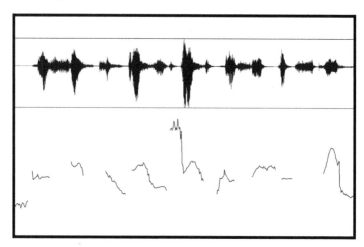

You will notice that the second graph demonstrates the way in which recognizing iambic pentameter as you speak holds the muscular sound of a line right the way through from start to finish. There is also more vocal range displayed here.

Of course we can't make artistic decisions based on a graph. But we can make some technical adjustments and we can get used to expanding our range of sound and the muscularity of our vocal delivery. If you have time at the end of this summary exercise, try going through the verse lines above once again, with a strong emphasis on the meter. As you do, see if you can begin to feel good about the sound of the meter. Relax with it, and play more in your sound generally. Sustain the vowels, and vary your pitch but keep the meter stresses. The more you use it and feel comfortable in the pattern, the easier it will be to incorporate it into your acting work.

Finding the bare bones of a speech

4 HOURS

This is the final analytical tool we need to acquire before we begin our work. Often when actors begin their work with Shakespeare, they can be overwhelmed. I've watched many performances where it is clear that the actor feels as if there is too much language, and that it is getting in the way of their acting.

When we talk about 'too much language', I think we are really referring to how complex Shakespeare's sentences are: he often uses long sentences with a lot of metaphorical descriptions and repetition. For this reason, the work can be overwhelming to read the first time. But remember that whenever we look at a sentence, no matter how long, no matter how complicated, we always find some simple grammatical things in order to make sense of it.

We need a *Subject* (who or what the sentence is about):

Jane

Then we need a *Verb* (an action or 'state of being' word):

Walks

This (a Subject and a Verb) is the very least information we need to make a sentence:

Jane walks.

We also usually have an *Object* (the thing that 'takes' the action):

Jane walks to the *store*.

Once we have these things we can understand what's going on – *we can follow the main action*. Of course, we can also do other things to the sentence. We can add things that aren't connected to the action. We can add modifiers like *Adjectives* (words that describe a noun or a pronoun):

> *Beautiful* **Jane walks to the store**.

We can add *Adverbs* (words that describe verbs)

> **Beautiful Jane walks *slowly* to the store.**

And of course, we can add more actions and more words to describe those actions:

> Beautiful, *but lazy*, Jane *shrugs off her afternoon haze and* walks *very deliberately, as if to irritate her mother, and as slowly as she possibly can* to the store, *where she* meets with her friends and wastes an hour *or so in the make-up aisle.*

Most of what we've added now is descriptive stuff. But in this very elaborate sentence above, we keep our concentration on the main *Subject/Verb/Object* combination in order to understand what is going on, and to follow the action. And although I've added a lot of extra description, I can put all this extra stuff into parentheses, and the bare bones of the sentence will still make sense. Read out just the bold words below:

> *(Beautiful, but lazy),* **Jane** *(shrugs off her afternoon haze and)* **walks** *(very deliberately, as if to irritate her mother, and as slowly as she possibly can)* **to the store**, *(where she)* **meets with** *(her)* **friends and wastes an hour** *(or so in the make-up aisle).*
>
> **Jane walks to the store, meets with friends and wastes an hour.**

The bare bones of our sentence follows the action and the rest of the sentence is now 'bracketed' off. Keep this bare bones idea in mind when you first approach a passage in Shakespeare and remember that finding, and concentrating on, subjects, verbs and objects will help you when faced with a lot of language you don't understand. This kind of analysis is useful in the early phase of your preparation because it not only helps you keep your eye on the action, it can help you figure out just what kind of monologue you are looking at, and whether this monologue is a good monologue for you. The exercise is also a great tool for discovering just how a monologue is structured, and that greatly aids clarity.

If you go back to look at the work in the box above, what you see is the bare bones of the sentence – it tells you, in the fewest words possible, what is going on. But beyond these bare bones, you can also see why an actor should <u>love all the stuff in the brackets</u>. That's right – the stuff that is often the scariest for an actor (and sometimes feels like 'too much language') is the very stuff that helps you make your acting choices. It is where we find out all the things we need to know about playing a given role. In the early stages of our work we need to see the bare bones, of course, because it takes us right to the heart of the action. But in terms of our work as actors, the 'parenthetical' phrases contain all the inspiring clues. For example, once we have identified the important action in our sentence above (Jane walks to the store, meets with friends, wastes an hour) we learn that:

- Jane is beautiful
- Jane is lazy
- Jane has a difficult/complex relationship with her mother
- Jane is probably young
- The afternoon is probably warm
- Jane likes make-up

These clues are helpful for us as actors in so many ways. As you see, most of what we've put in brackets is descriptive, and these descriptions immediately have an impact on our physical choices and they give us some general but very helpful ideas about who Jane is.

This kind of bare bones and 'parenthetical' or 'bracketed' phrase analysis works well in Shakespeare's text, because it helps us to keep our eye on the action initially, and that is exactly what our audience needs to focus on in order to make sense of the play. Let's look at some examples that will help to make this analysis easier for you to understand and then do.

Example 1

This is another very long sentence, and instead of talking about Jane, it is the character of Hotspur from **Henry IV**, talking about a particularly annoying messenger sent from the King:

> But I remember, when the fight was done,
> When I was dry with rage, and extreme toil,
> Breathless and faint, leaning upon my sword,
> Came there a certain lord, neat and trimly dress'd,
> Fresh as a bridegroom, and his chin new-reape'd
> Show'd like a stubble-land at harvest-home.

This is a long sentence, but there aren't many things to confuse us. The style may not be contemporary but it isn't hard to work out what is being said. We need to find the subject ('I' – Hotspur himself), verbs ('remember', 'was dry' 'came'), and object (the 'Lord' that Hotspur remembers). From these simple things we can work out a 'bare bones' version. In other words, we can find the least number of words that will still convey the meaning and the action. Once we know who is doing what to whom, we then just temporarily bracket out description or repetition:

> (But) **I remember, when the fight was done**,
> When I was dry with rage, and extreme toil,
> Breathless and faint, leaning upon my sword),
> **Came there a certain lord**, (neat and trimly dress'd,
> Fresh as a bridegroom, and his chin new-reape'd
> Show'd like a stubble-land at harvest-home.)
> **I remember, when the fight was done, came there a certain lord.**

This little bare bone version is a bit like 'Jane walks' above, but it is in a strange order. To contemporary ears it would sound clearer to say:

I remember, when the fight was done, a certain Lord came there.

But even in Shakespeare's language, we can understand it easily, and it is a full sentence. It doesn't tell us much except it does follow the main action of the speech, which is, simply, that Hotspur remembers seeing a Lord on the battlefield right after the fight. But this brief 'bare bone' sentence demonstrates in a graphic way that this sentence contains a lot more description than action. In fact, there are forty-nine words in the sentence and only twelve describe the immediate action. And that action is very simple: Hotspur remembers seeing a Lord after the battle. But to find out why we have so much language around this simple action, we need to go back and look at what's left in the 'parenthetical' phrases. Once we identify the fact that Hotspur sees a lord, the descriptive language tells us that Hotspur is:

- Dry with rage
- Angry
- Extremely tired
- breathless
- faint
- leaning on his sword

And we learn that the Lord is:

- Neat
- Trim
- Fresh
- Newly shaved

We know now that the action – remembering seeing a lord – isn't as important as the description of the scene. If we didn't do any other work on this sentence, we would already know quite a lot about how to play this sentence by having done this exercise. And even without knowing that Hotspur is so nicknamed because he has a quick and violent temper, we would imagine that this meeting between the battle-wearied Hotspur and the rather too carefully groomed Lord is NOT going to go well.

Separating the bare bones from the rest of the text also helps us to understand a lot more about what is going on with the character, and what kind of monologue it is. This sentence is unusual for Hotspur, because it contains far more description than action.

We are going to take four more examples here, which I think will help you to see how the bare bones exercise will do much more for you than just help you focus on the action.

Example 2

This is Ophelia's speech in *Hamlet*, in Act 3, Scene 1:

> O, what a noble mind is here o'erthrown!
> The courtier's, soldier's, scholar's, eye, tongue, sword,
> Th'expectancy and rose of the fair state,
> The glass of fashion and the mould of form,
> Th'observed of all observers, quite, quite, down!
> And I, of ladies most deject and wretched,
> That sucked the honey of his music vows,
> Now see that noble and most sovereign reason
> Like sweet bells, jangled, out of time and harsh,
> That unmatch'd form and feature of blown youth
> Blasted with ecstasy. O, woe is me
> T'have seen what I have seen, see what I see!

Look up any words you don't know, and don't focus too much on anything that is confusing you. Just follow the action, and bracket off the description. Here is what I think are the bare bones of the speech with the descriptive or repetitive parts of the text in parentheses:

O, what a (noble) **mind is** (here) **o'erthrown!**
(The courtier's, soldier's, scholar's, eye, tongue, sword,

Th'expectancy and rose of the fair state,
The glass of fashion and the mould of form,)
Th'observed of all observers (is)[1] (quite,) **quite, down!**
And I, (of ladies most deject and wretched,
That sucked the honey of his music vows,)
Now see that (noble and most sovereign) **reason**
(Like sweet bells)**, jangled,** (out of time and harsh,)
That (unmatch'd) **form** (and feature) **of** (blown) **youth**
Blasted (with ecstasy. O,) **woe is me**
T'have seen what I have seen, see what I see!

Now we have the bare bones of the speech that follows the action, and it is very clear what's going on. Ophelia has seen Hamlet behaving as if he's lost his mind, and as if he no longer loves her. Ophelia's main action is to describe her shock at the terrible change she sees in him – in the final line she compares what she *has* seen of him before, and what he looks like now.

As you look at the speech above, what would you say is roughly the balance between bare bones and 'parenthetical' language? It is always important to try to have a rough idea of that balance. You can see that it is not equal (50/50). In fact, if you count the words, you find that it is about 35 per cent bare bones or language that focuses on what's going on, and 65 per cent is descriptive or repetitive. That makes this monologue a largely descriptive one, and describing what she's just seen is Ophelia's main action.

When you are doing a bare bones analysis of a text, your aim is to make the most sense of what's going on with the fewest words that you can. And we can see that the bare bones speech, with description and repetition now left out, makes perfect sense. So why the extra language? Well, if you think back to our first sentence about Jane, you'll remember that the 'extra language' gave us a lot of clues about character and world. So let's have a look at Ophelia's 'extra words', in order. Start by reading these aloud:

- Noble
- The courtier's, soldier's, scholar's, eye, tongue, sword

---

[1] You'll see I've added a word here to help make sense of the sentence.

- Th'expectancy and rose of the fair state
- The glass of fashion and the mould of form
- of ladies most deject and wretched
- noble and most sovereign
- Sweet bells, out of time and harsh

When I look at these words, I feel as if they amount to a kind of summary of Ophelia's world: nobility, the Court, fashion, expectancy (of youth), Sovereignty, etc. They say so much about Ophelia's physical world and about what makes Ophelia who she is. We are highly unlikely to call someone 'the rose of the fair state' or compare their intellect to 'sweet bells'. But this language comes naturally to Ophelia, who understands why Hamlet was the rose of the state and why sweet bells are both beautiful and comforting in her world.

Metaphor comes easily to her, which means she is probably an educated young woman, and all of her metaphors are about flowers, form and music. As a young noble woman of the court, her life would centre much around such things: flowers, form, and music. That means it is the 'extra', 'parenthetical' words and phrases that bring the speech to life, and give you all the clues as to who Ophelia IS, and what her world is like.

Example 3

This example is a <u>tough</u> speech of Berowne's from *Love's Labour's Lost* (don't spend time worrying about understanding it all – just have a read through and focus on what you CAN understand):

Thus pour the stars down plagues for perjury.
Can any face of brass hold longer out?
Here stand I. lady, dart thy skill at me;
Bruise me with scorn, confound me with a flout;
Thrust thy sharp wit quite through my ignorance;
Cut me to pieces with thy keen conceit;
And I will wish thee never more to dance,
Nor never more in Russian habit wait.

O, never will I trust to speeches penn'd,
Nor to the motion of a schoolboy's tongue,
Nor never come in vizard to my friend,
Nor woo in rhyme, like a blind harper's song!
Taffeta phrases, silken terms precise,
Three-piled hyperboles, spruce affectation,
Figures pedantical; these summer-flies
Have blown me full of maggot ostentation:
I do forswear them; and I here protest,
By this white glove; – how white the hand, God knows! –
Henceforth my wooing mind shall be express'd
In russet yeas and honest kersey noes:
And, to begin, wench,– so God help me, la! –
My love to thee is sound, sans crack or flaw.

I've chosen this speech because I think it is exactly the sort of speech that frightens most people when they first start working with Shakespeare's language. On first reading it may seem that there are so many things NOT to understand here. Rather than focus on those difficult things, let's go through and focus on what's going on. Don't spend time trying too hard to understand things in this early phase, but do find out what the more difficult words – 'flout', 'vizard', 'figures pedantical', 'maggot ostentation' – mean by putting them into the search on www.shakespeareswords.com. Once you've done that, put any descriptive or repetitive phrases in parentheses, and see if you can work out what is going on here. Do this now before you look at my suggestions below.

Here is my version of the bare bones of the speech. I've put repetitions and descriptions in parentheses:

Thus pour the stars down plagues for perjury.
Can any face of brass hold longer out?
Here stand I. Lady, (dart thy skill at me)
Bruise me with *scorn*, (confound me with a flout;
Thrust thy sharp wit quite through my ignorance;
Cut me to pieces with thy keen conceit);
And I will wish thee never more to dance,
(Nor never more in Russian habit wait.)

O, never will I trust to speeches penn'd,
(Nor to the motion of a schoolboy's tongue,
Nor never come in vizard to my friend,
Nor woo in rhyme, like a blind harper's song!
Taffeta phrases, silken terms precise,
Three-piled hyperboles, spruce affectation,
Figures pedantical; these summer-flies
Have blown me full of maggot ostentation:
I do forswear them) **and I here protest,**
By this white glove; (– how white the hand, God knows! –
Henceforth my wooing mind shall be express'd
In russet yeas and honest kersey noes:)
(And, to begin, wench) – **so God help me,** (la!) –
My love to thee is sound, (sans crack or flaw)

As you see, in the first 'parenthetical' section he's repeating ways that she can 'bruise him', then he makes a pretty repetitive list of all the things he will never do again, and finally he repeats and describes his vow ('protest'). These are the sections I've bracketed out.

Now in this 'bare' version, this speech is much clearer. What is also clear is how much language Berowne uses that is above and beyond the bare action. Now, admittedly, we still may not understand everything in these lines, because we haven't read the whole play and we are just looking at this speech out of context. But even so, we can almost certainly understand what these bare bones mean – particularly because we've left out so much:

Thus pour the stars down plagues for perjury *(We always get punished for lying)*
Can any face of brass hold longer out? *(Could a more shameless person carry on any longer?)*
Here stand I. Lady *(Here I am, Lady)*
Bruise me with scorn *(Be as mean to me as you like)*
And I will wish thee never more to dance *(I won't bother asking you to dance)*
O, never will I trust to speeches *(I won't make flattering talk)*
and I here protest, By this white glove *(and I swear by this glove)*

so God help me, My love to thee is sound, *(by God, I love you truly)*

Now that you've seen a bare bones version – what would you say is the balance of action to description here? If you actually count, you'll see that there is only about 30 per cent of the speech that is centred on the immediate action (inviting her to abuse him, swearing that he won't ask her to dance or make speeches, swearing his love to her). That leaves a whopping 70 per cent of the speech that either is repetitive, or centres on description. That makes this speech a feast of language – it is going to serve an actor who loves that; an actor who relishes language, and can find a lot of colour, expressiveness and joy in the playing.

But what might we say is Berowne's main action here? There could be many answers to that, but I think it is two-fold: he wants to admit that his approach to Rosaline has been all wrong and, then, to declare his true love for her. But because he has spent so much time on elaborate language and description, I think there may be a third action: I think he wants to use language the way a peacock uses its feathers – as a dazzling sexual display activity.

I've deliberately chosen a pretty tough speech here – I find the whole of *Love's Labour's Lost* pretty hard. Not all of Shakespeare is this tough, but I hope that starting with a tough one first will help to prove my point. Focus first on following the action you can understand, and find the bare bones of the speech in those parts. Underline it, '**BOLD**' it as I did above, or simply write it out separately from the rest of the text and then have a look at it.

One of the purposes of looking at the bare bones of a speech is that it allows you to get any monologue into a form where you will probably be able to sum up what it is about very quickly. This tough speech boils down to some simple action: Berowne is apologizing for trying to be too witty/clever in expressing his love. He invites her to insult him for being so foolish and swears to be more straightforward and simply confess his feeling. But *does* he do that?

Now that we understand the essence of the speech, we can go back to look at what all the stuff in the 'parenthetical' phrases might mean. While we may not know the play yet, we DO know quite a lot at this point, just from getting to the bare bones:

- Berowne uses a LOT of language, and much of it is repetitive
- He calls himself 'ignorant' when clearly he is not
- He says he will never more 'trust' 'speeches' and then goes on to make quite a speech
- He declares that he will express himself in honest 'yes or no' terms, then goes on to swear his love with a poetical turn of phrase: 'sans crack or flaw'

The job of an actor is continually to make choices. And given what we know so far, we can probably begin to make some early choices about who Berowne is from this exercise on one monologue. Once we get past the action, we look at all the 'extra' speech and we can surmise that Berowne is:

- Intelligent and very well educated
- His main metaphors are to do with swordfighting (lines 3, 4, 5); school ('schoolboy' 'pedantical') and expensive cloth ('taffeta' 'silk') – surely his world is largely composed of schoolrooms, fencing lessons and fine clothes?
- Contradicting himself (possibly he's nervous?)
- Quite inexperienced in love (and therefore probably young?)
- Probably high-status and possibly powerful (he is allowed to go on and on in this speech, and it is clear he doesn't anticipate interruption)
- Confident, despite the self-deprecating sound of this speech

This early work on our speech has led us to quite a bit of knowledge about Berowne and the world he inhabits. We still have work to do (read/watch the play or at least get a good synopsis to begin with), but we should feel much more confident about approaching this speech now.

This is one of the reasons to separate the bare bones of a speech from the rest of the language in Shakespeare: it helps us figure out the difference between the words that make the action of the speech clear, and the words that make the character, the world or the situation clear. Often when we don't understand Shakespeare in performance, it is because the actor hasn't learned how to make sure that, whatever vocal fireworks we may bring to the descriptive/metaphorical/repetitive language, the audience hears clearly the bare bones – which is usually where the most substantial part of the ACTION lies. At this point, we also have a little knowledge about whether this is the kind of speech (which has a majority of descriptive language) that will play to our acting strengths … or not!

Example 4

Our last example is a very different experience – this is Hotspur once again. On the eve of battle, he has received a very distressing letter from his father:

> Sick now! droop now! this sickness doth infect
> The very life-blood of our enterprise;
> 'Tis catching hither, even to our camp.
> He writes me here, that inward sickness–
> And that his friends by deputation could not
> So soon be drawn, nor did he think it meet
> To lay so dangerous and dear a trust
> On any soul removed but on his own.
> Yet doth he give us bold advertisement,
> That with our small conjunction we should on,
> To see how fortune is disposed to us;
> For, as he writes, there is no quailing now.
> Because the king is certainly possess'd
> Of all our purposes. What say you to it?

If we bracket the descriptive or repetitive words or phrases first, we get to the bare bones pretty quickly:

> **Sick now!** (droop now!) **this sickness doth infect**
> (The very life-blood of) **our enterprise**;
> ('Tis catching hither, even to our camp.)
> **He writes me** (here,) **(of)** (that inward) **sickness** –
> **And that his friends** (by deputation) **could not**

So soon be drawn, nor did he think it meet
To lay so dangerous (and dear) **a trust**
On any soul (removed) **but on his own.**
Yet doth he give us (bold) **advertisement,**
That (with our small conjunction) **we should (go) on,**
To see how fortune is disposed to us;
For, as he writes, there is no quailing now.
Because the king is (certainly) **possess'd**
Of all **our purposes. What say you to it?**

Before we have even had a chance to consider this short monologue, we can immediately note a big difference between this Hotspur monologue and the brief Hotspur lines we considered earlier. And, of course, there's a massive difference here between this and Berowne's monologue. What would you guess is the balance of 'bare bone' action and description here? In fact about 75 per cent is necessary to make the meaning and the action clear. That leaves only about 25 per cent that is descriptive.

In the more descriptive Hotspur sentence we looked at on page 52, he was at court, recalling a moment that had happened earlier, and he wanted to describe exactly why the lord who had appeared on the battlefield irritated him so much. Consequently, that speech has a lot more description than action. But in this speech, Hotspur is right in the heat of danger. He has decided to lead a rebellion against the king and was awaiting the support of his father's troops to swell his rebel's ranks. Instead, he receives a letter that says his father is not coming. His main action now is two-fold: he needs to tell his comrades that the old man isn't coming and he needs to know if his comrades in arms think that his father is right – should they go on without those extra troops because to do otherwise is dangerous? He needs answers. He doesn't have time for much description, and he doesn't have much time for metaphor, so he only uses one – he compares his rebellion to a body – which needs its 'life-blood' and in that metaphor he sees his father's sickness as infecting the whole body of the rebellion.

Please understand that I am NOT suggesting that there are 'extra' words or 'parenthetical' words that aren't as important as the others. All the language is important. But in the early stages of work, it will help you to shape meaning if you can get right to the bare bones of action when you can. Once you done that, you can focus your energy on the bare bones first, and then see what you can gather from what's left – what is the main action? How does the parenthetical language 'sound'? Can you find any strong metaphorical themes? What kind of metaphors or imagery do you find – and what might those metaphors suggest about the world that the character inhabits? Here, Hotspur's strong metaphor about 'life-blood' and about his rebellion being a body tells you much about what's on Hotspur's mind at this dangerous moment: blood and bodies. Remember that much of the joy of your acting will lie in what you discover in the 'parenthetical' language.

We are going to be using this bare bones analysis when choosing and preparing your monologue, so it is worth doing some exercises to help you feel confident with it.

EXERCISE 1

We are just going to start with some short passages to allow some practice on getting to the bare bones of a piece, and we'll work our way up to longer, more challenging pieces. Keep in mind that the whole point of creating a bare bones version of a monologue is not only to help you focus on what is going on in the monologue, and on what your audience needs to hear, but also to ensure that you understand the structure of the monologue.

Put parentheses around descriptive or repetitive words/phrases that aren't needed to make sense of the action or meaning in these shorter passages. As you do this, please remember that there is no right or wrong here – a bare bones version will always be the result of what you think is most important. Suggested answers are at the end of this section.

I.

If music be the food of love, play on –
Give me excess of it, that, surfeiting,
The appetite may sicken, and so die.

II.

She made good view of me – indeed so much
That methought her eyes had lost her tongue
For she did speak in starts distractedly.

III.

On each side her
Stood pretty dimpled boys, like smiling Cupids,
With divers-coloured fans, whose wind did seem
To glow the delicate cheeks which they did cool …

IV.

These are the forgeries of jealousy:
And never since the middle summer's spring
Met we on hill, in dale, forest or mead,
By paved fountain or by rushy brook,
Or in the beached margent of the sea
To dance our ringlets to the whistling wind,
But with thy brawls thou has disturbed our sport.

EXERCISE 2

*This is a monologue by the Earl of Worcester. It follows Hotspur's
decision to go ahead and challenge the King in battle without his father.
But King Henry has asked for a discussion first. Hotspur sends Worcester
and Vernon to speak with the King, and Henry has made what looks
like a very generous offer if Hotspur will stand his troops down. On the
way back to the rebel camp, Vernon is keen to tell Hotspur of the King's
generous offer, but Worcester doesn't trust the King:*

Then are we all undone.
It is not possible, it cannot be,
The king should keep his word in loving us.
He will suspect us still and find a time
To punish this offence in other faults.
Suspicion all our lives shall be stuck full of eyes;
For treason is but trusted like the fox,
Who, ne'er so tame, so cherished and locked up,
Will have a wild trick of his ancestors.
Look how we can, or sad or merrily,
Interpretation will misquote our looks,
And we shall feed like oxen at a stall,
The better cherished still the nearer death.
My nephew's trespass may be well forgot;
it hath the excuse of youth and heat of blood,
And an adopted name of privilege,
A hare-brained Hotspur, governed by a spleen.
All his offences live upon my head
And on his father's. We did train him on,
And, his corruption being ta'en from us,
We, as the spring of all, shall pay for all.
Therefore, good cousin, let not Harry know,
In any case, the offer of the king.

First, simply concentrate on everything you DO understand and look up any word you don't understand. Put descriptive and repetitive things in brackets.

What is Worcester's main action?

_____

What is the balance of bare bones to 'parenthetical' language here?

_____

What do you make of the parenthetical words and phrases here?
Any strong imagery or metaphors? Do these tell you anything about
Worcester or his world?

_____

_____

EXERCISE 3

This monologue is delivered by Queen Margaret, who is also on the
battlefield, and trying to inspire her soldiers to stop feeling defeated
by the deaths of so many of their generals. As before, concentrate
on everything you DO understand and look up any word you don't
understand. Once you've done that, put all descriptive and repetitive
parts in brackets.

> Great lords, wise men ne'er sit and wail their loss,
> But cheerly seek how to redress their harms.
> What though the mast be now blown overboard,
> The cable broke, the holding-anchor lost,
> And half our sailors swallow'd in the flood?
> Yet lives our pilot still. Is't meet that he
> Should leave the helm and like a fearful lad
> With tearful eyes add water to the sea
> And give more strength to that which hath too much,
> Whiles, in his moan, the ship splits on the rock,
> Which industry and courage might have saved?
> Ah, what a shame! ah, what a fault were this!
> Say Warwick was our anchor; what of that?
> And Montague our topmost; what of him?
> Our slaughter'd friends the tackles; what of these?
> Why, is not Oxford here another anchor?
> And Somerset another goodly mast?

The friends of France our shrouds and tacklings?
And, though unskilful, why not Ned and I
For once allow'd the skilful pilot's charge?
We will not from the helm to sit and weep,
But keep our course, though the rough wind say no ...

Now answer these questions:
What is Margaret's main action here?

_____

What is the balance of bare bones to 'parenthetical' language here?

_____

What do you make of the parenthetical words and phrases here? Any strong imagery or metaphors? Do these tell you anything about Margaret or her world?

_____

_____

_____

_____

COMPLETED EXAMPLES OF EXERCISES 1, 2 AND 3

Here are my bare bone versions of the short passages in Exercise 1. Again, remember that there are no absolutes of right or wrong here – there are many ways to do these exercises.

I.

If music be the food of love, play on –
Give me excess of it, that, (surfeiting,)
The appetite may (sicken, and so) die.

I think almost all the words are necessary to the meaning here, but I can imagine that someone might create this version:

If music be the food of love, play on –
(Give me excess of it) that (surfeiting,)
The appetite may (sicken, and so) die.

II.

She made good view of me – (indeed) so much
(That) methought her eyes had lost her tongue
For she did speak (in starts) distractedly.

I think about 90 per cent of the words are necessary to the meaning here, but I can imagine that someone might create this version:

She made good view of me – (indeed so much
That methought her eyes had lost her tongue)
For she did speak (in starts) distractedly.

III.

On each side her
Stood (pretty dimpled) boys, (like smiling Cupids,)
With (divers-coloured) fans, whose wind did seem
To glow the (delicate) cheeks (which) they did cool …

I think about 75 per cent of the words are necessary to the meaning here, but the overall passage is so descriptive that perhaps someone might prefer:

On each side her
Stood (pretty dimpled) **boys,** (like smiling Cupids,)
With (divers-coloured) **fans,** (whose wind did seem
To glow the delicate cheeks which they did cool …)

IV.
These are (the) **forgeries** (of jealousy)
And never since (the) **middle summer**('s spring)
Met we (on hill, in dale, forest or mead,
By paved fountain or by rushy brook,
Or in the beached margent of the sea)
To dance (our ringlets to the whistling wind),
But (with thy brawls) **thou has disturbed our sport.**

I think only about 20 per cent of the words are necessary to the meaning here, but you might keep some phrases ('of jealousy'? 'with thy brawls'?).

This is my bare bone version of the Exercise 2 monologue:

Then are we (all) **undone.**
It is not possible, (it cannot be),
The king should keep his word (in loving us).
He will suspect us (still) **and** (find a time
To) **punish this offence** (in other faults).
Suspicion all our lives shall be stuck full of eyes;
(For treason is but trusted like the fox,
Who, ne'er so tame, so cherished and locked up,
Will have a wild trick of his ancestors.)
Look how we can, (or sad or merrily),
Interpretation will misquote our looks,
(And we shall feed like oxen at a stall,
The better cherished still the nearer death.)
My nephew's trespass may be well forgot;

> it hath the excuse of youth (and heat of blood,
> And an adopted name of privilege,
> A hare-brained Hotspur, governed by a spleen.)
> All his offences live upon my head
> And on his father's. We did train him on,
> And, (his corruption being ta'en from us,)
> We, as the spring of all, shall pay for all.
> Therefore, good cousin, let not Harry know,
> In any case, the offer of the king.

Again, you may not entirely agree with my version – and that's okay. All that matters is that your bare bones retains the sense of the speech. The balance of bare bones speech to the whole speech here is about 60/40. Some of the parenthetical phrases aren't description, but they are repetitive and serve to emphasize Worcester's point: just how dangerous it would be to tell Harry that the King has made a good offer to them if they abandon the rebellion.

What is Worcester's main action?

He wants to convince Vernon that if they accept the King's offer their lives will be miserable and the King will ultimately take his revenge on them.

What is the balance of bare bones to 'parenthetical' language here?

The bare bones make up about 60 per cent of the speech.

What do you make of the parenthetical words and phrases here? Any strong imagery or metaphors? Do these tell you anything about Worcester or his world?

The lengthy metaphors are about animals (fox, hare and oxen) – which tells me that Worcester sees himself in a world where people hunt and kill each other and dog-eat-dog is the rule. It also tells me that Worcester sees that humans revert to their animal instincts when danger is in the air.

Here is my 'bare bone' version of the Exercise 3 monologue:

Great lords, wise men ne'er (sit and) wail their loss,

But (cheerly) seek (how) to redress their harms.
What though the mast be now blown overboard,
(The cable broke, the holding-anchor lost,)
And half our sailors swallow'd in the flood?
Yet lives our pilot still. Is't meet that he
Should leave the helm (and like a fearful lad
With tearful eyes add water to the sea
And give more strength to that which hath too much,)
Whiles, (in his moan), the ship splits on the rock,
Which (industry and) courage might have saved?
Ah, what a shame! (ah, what a fault were this!)
Say Warwick was our anchor; what of that?
(And Montague our topmost; what of him?
Our slaughter'd friends the tackles; what of these?)
Why, is not Oxford here another anchor?
(And Somerset another goodly mast?
The friends of France our shrouds and tacklings?)
And, (though unskillful), why not Ned and I
(For once) allow'd the (skillful) pilot's charge?
We will not (from the helm to) sit and weep,
But keep our course, though the rough wind say no…

What is Margaret's main action here?
    She wants to stop her soldiers from wailing over their defeat and she
    wants them to allow her and her son to become the head of the army.

What is the balance of bare bones to 'parenthetical' language here?
    The bare bones make up about 55 per cent of the speech. Like
    Hotspur, earlier, Margaret is in the heat of battle here and she needs
    to inspire her drooping soldiers and to gain their confidence in her
    leadership.

*What do you make of the parenthetical words and phrases here? Any
strong imagery or metaphors? Do these tell you anything about Margaret
or her world?*
    She uses a lengthy 'wrecked ship' metaphor – very possibly because

in England, monarchs usually saw the greatest threat as coming from across the Channel. She repeats herself and adds more examples than one might usually, because she clearly thinks the soldiers need a lot of inspiration. She might also be trying to inspire herself and it is clear that she feels she needs to work very hard at this moment to rally the troops, and perhaps thinks that if she makes the speech strong enough the soldiers will see her as their natural leader.

At this point you should feel confident about creating a quick bare bones analysis of a monologue. We'll be using this technique once we get into Phase 2.

Imagining action

3 HOURS

The final skill we need to practice is the ability to imagine a detailed, active world all round us when performing. This is a purely creative exercise, which is always inspired by the text but not tied to it. In other words, we start with what IS happening in the speech, and then we go on to create two things:

1   A whole world of possible things that MIGHT BE happening as we speak.

2   A plan of all the ways in which we want to change or affect what we are seeing or who we are speaking to.

Of course, if we were doing a full production, we would have spent many weeks with other actors and a director and all of these choices would have been made within the company, discussed and rehearsed many times. But as you are working alone, you have to create the imagined world by yourself. This takes time and inventiveness, but will result in an experience that significantly lessens self-consciousness as you perform. Working even in the very early stages of preparation by filling your imagination with life and detail will train your focus outward onto the world and the people that you want to have an impact on, and can greatly alleviate the sense of isolation that auditioning actors often feel. In the first phase – the learning process – we want as much action as we can imagine, both mental and physical. Just as important as what we are seeing around us, and how we might move in this imagined world, is knowing who we are talking to and what we think they are feeling/thinking about us. It is right here – in our desire to **change how they are feeling/thinking** – that all of our acting choices take place.

A neat example of this would be to imagine how differently, as Lady Percy, you would play the opening of her monologue if you imagined first that Hotspur was looking angry with you and drawing his sword, and then imagined that he was smiling at you and unbuttoning his shirt. In either case you would want him to stop and listen to you, but your energy and tactics would change significantly between these two scenarios. All your acting decisions are going to rely on what you see him doing/feeling/thinking, and on what you WANT him to do/feel/think.

We need some specific examples, so let's start with a brief excerpt from the Duke in **As You Like It**:

> Now, my co-mates and brothers in exile,
> Hath not old custom made this life more sweet
> Than that of painted pomp? Are not these woods
> More free from peril than the envious court?

We can quickly imagine what he is seeing: he sees his exiled friends, and he is in the woods. So we know where he is and who he is talking to. But for our purposes, this isn't enough. We need to create action, and more detail that will help us both in our learning process and in our performance process. Here is what I might come up with for these first four lines:

Text	Action	Speaking to?
	I look around and see that my exiled colleagues are looking cold, tired and depressed. I've poured some wine in our glasses and I raise mine to them. I see the sun shining through a sparkling canopy of leaves as I look up, and I want them to look up too.	Amiens, 1st and 2nd Lord
Now, my co-mates and brothers in exile, Hath not old custom made this life more sweet Than that of painted pomp? Are not these woods More free from peril than the envious court?	*I notice that the 2nd Lord is looking particularly sad so I put down my glass, step toward him, and address the 2nd question to him. I want him to smile.*	2nd Lord

As you can see, I've written in both my physical actions – looking up at the sun through the trees, raising my glass for a toast, putting it down and stepping toward the 2nd Lord – and my thoughts about what I see and what I want to see. You'll notice that I haven't mentioned my feelings. When you are writing out your action in this way, *always keep your feelings out of it.*

The next example is Cleopatra at the moment when Antony dies:

> Noblest of men, woo't die?
> Hast thou no care of me? Shall I abide
> In this dull world, which in thy absence is
> No better than a sty? O, see, my women, [ANTONY *dies*]
> The crown o' the earth doth melt.

Again, we know who she's talking to and we know from the play that her women are with her, and that the fatally wounded Antony has been brought before her. That gives us a lot of material for creating the imagined world and the physical action of these five lines.

Text	Action	Speaking to?
	I watch two men with frightened faces bring Antony's body in and lay it down before me. I see blood on his chest and instinctively lay my hand on it to stop the bleeding. I look to his face and see how beautiful he is.	
Noblest of men, woo't die? Hast thou no care of me? shall I abide In this dull world, which in thy absence is No better than a sty?	*I put my hands on both sides of his face and turn his look onto me. He needs to see me – I know I can keep him alive.*	Antony
O, see, my women, [ANTONY dies]	*His eyes close and I know. I pull my hands away from his face. I can't bear to feel that skin grow cold.*	Charmian and Iras

Text	Action	Speaking to?
	I look to Charmian and Iras – they look horrified. I look at the blood on my hand.	
The crown o' the earth doth melt.	*I look back to Antony and I want to touch him, but I don't want to feel cold skin.*	Antony

Of course, the way we imagine this world, and the physical actions we give ourselves will be a pretty subjective thing. Every actor interprets differently – that's why we can watch *Hamlet* over and over again: we want to see what a different actor will do with the part. But however you imagine things, you absolutely must include physical action, and you must see the faces and the actions of the person/s you are speaking to. Be very specific in all of this.

We'll look at one more example before trying the exercises. This is the young convent virgin, Isabella, in **Measure for Measure**. The all-powerful Angelo has threatened to torture and kill her brother if she does not submit to his desire for her, and although this reveals Angelo to be a villain, he is respected and thought highly virtuous by all in Vienna. As he leaves her, she realizes that no one will take her word over his:

> To whom should I complain? Did I tell this,
> Who would believe me? O perilous mouths,
> That bear in them one and the self-same tongue,
> Either of condemnation or approof;
> Bidding the law make court'sy to their will:
> Hooking both right and wrong to the appetite,
> To follow as it draws! I'll to my brother:
> Though he hath fallen by prompture of the blood,
> Yet hath he in him such a mind of honour.
> That, had he twenty heads to tender down
> On twenty bloody blocks, he'ld yield them up,
> Before his sister should her body stoop
> To such abhorr'd pollution.

> Then, Isabel, live chaste, and, brother, die:

More than our brother is our chastity.
I'll tell him yet of Angelo's request,
And fit his mind to death, for his soul's rest.

This is a soliloquy – which means that she is speaking on stage with no other characters around her. Actors often perform soliloquys as if they are talking to themselves, but with rare exception (and the last few lines of this monologue are one of those exceptions), you will always be more active and more exciting if you can imagine you are speaking to someone. Here is my version of what is happening during Isabella speech:

Text	Action	Speaking to?
To whom should I complain? Did I tell this, Who would believe me?	I watch the door close as Angelo goes out and I look to heaven. The silence is overwhelming. I need an answer, so I kneel down and I ask these questions sincerely, but nothing comes.	God
O perilous mouths, That bear in them one and the self-same tongue, Either of condemnation or approof; Bidding the law make court'sy to their will: Hooking both right and wrong to the appetite, To follow as it draws!	I can see Angelo's leering face in front of me and now I think of all the things I wish I'd said to him while he was in the room. I stand up to face him and I say them to him now, hoping to shame him into mercy. His face stays the same – laughing at me, looking lustfully at me. I keep trying to make that change.	Angelo
I'll to my brother: Though he hath fallen by prompture of the blood, Yet hath he in him such a mind of honour. That, had he twenty heads to tender down On twenty bloody blocks, he'ld yield them up, Before his sister should her body stoop To such abhorr'd pollution.	I'm lost for a moment, but then I imagine my Mother Superior from the convent and I know what she would say. She would tell me to have faith in God and in my brother. I let her know that she is right – she believes the best of my brother, and so should I. As I speak, I can see that she approves of my faith in god and in my brother's goodness. And in her strength and faith I am reminded that it is God's mercy that is important. I make her smile in approval of my decision.	Mother Superior

Text	Action	Speaking to?
Then, Isabel, live chaste, and, brother, die: More than our brother is our chastity. I'll tell him yet of Angelo's request, And fit his mind to death, for his soul's rest.	*There is a mirror on the wall in front of me. I step toward it. I see that I look shaken. I look myself in the eye and make myself remember God's mercy and the fact that what has happened is all part of God's plan for me and for Claudio.*	My reflection

Creating this detailed world and planning your physical action is critical in the learning phase of the monologue, but you won't keep all the physical action in performance. Once you get to the later phases of rehearsal you will start refining the physical action, and it may be that in performance you won't keep any of the physical movement. But while you are learning, the physical action is a way of getting your body involved in the monologue. Even if you go on eventually to cut out all of the physical movement, having rehearsed it in the early stages helps you feel more physically connected with your imagined world and is an aid to memory.

EXERCISE 1

We'll finish this section on skills acquisition with some exercises in imagining action. Of course there are no 'right' answers for these exercises, but at the end of the section you can find what I think are some possible ways to imagine the world of these speeches. We'll start with the first few lines of Romeo's monologue in Act 3, Scene 3. This is a relatively simple exercise, because where know where Romeo is (he is in Friar Laurence's cell – a small, poor room) and we know who he is speaking to (Friar Laurence):

'Tis torture, and not mercy: heaven is here,
Where Juliet lives; and every cat and dog
And little mouse, every unworthy thing,
Live here in heaven and may look on her;
But Romeo may not:

Of course, if you did this speech in a production of the play, you would know exactly what you were seeing. There would be a set, and an actor playing Friar Laurence. But as you are doing this for audition, you must provide all of that through your imagination alone.

Text	Action	Speaking to?
'Tis torture, and not mercy: heaven is here, Where Juliet lives; and every cat and dog And little mouse, every unworthy thing, Live here in heaven and may look on her; But Romeo may not:		

EXERCISE 2

This is the slightly more difficult opening of Sebastian's monologue in Act 4, Scene 3, because we know where he is (Olivia's garden) but we don't know who he's speaking to. This is a soliloquy, because it is spoken by an actor on stage alone:

This is the air; that is the glorious sun;
This pearl she gave me, I do feel't and see't;
And though 'tis wonder that enwraps me thus,
Yet 'tis not madness. Where's Antonio, then?
I could not find him at the Elephant:

Yet there he was; and there I found this credit,
That he did range the town to seek me out.
His counsel now might do me golden service;

In Shakespeare's production (as in most modern productions), the actor
playing Sebastian would speak directly to the audience, doing his best
to explain to them why he's is such a state of confusion. In an audition
situation, this gives the actor some problems. Most people advise
against playing to an audition panel. But with a speech like this, I think
it is fine, as long as you imagine that the panel are only part of a huge
audience. That means you keep your gaze moving among all the faces
you see – both those that are actually in the room, and those that are in
the audience of your imagination.

SOME POSSIBLE ANSWERS FOR EXERCISES 1 AND 2

Exercise 1

Text	Action	Speaking to?
	The Friar is furious with me for not welcoming banishment. He doesn't understand why the sentence is horrible to me, and I don't care if he's angry. I have to explain it so that he WILL understand and I have to make him shut up about the Prince	
'Tis torture, and not mercy: heaven is here, Where Juliet lives; and every cat and dog	being merciful.	Friar Laurence
And little mouse, every unworthy thing, Live here in heaven and may look on her;	I see a movement out of the corner of my eye – there's a mouse running along the floor and I grab an apple from the Friar's desk and throw it at him.	The mouse!

Text	Action	Speaking to?
But Romeo may not:	*I see Juliet's sleeping face on the pillow of her bed. She looks so beautiful. But I must tell her what's happened and I take a step toward the bed.*	Juliet

This might feel like a LOT of action for a very few lines, but when I tried it out in rehearsal, I liked the feeling of throwing an apple at a mouse. It felt good. I also liked imagining Juliet's face. Your version may be much simpler. You have to experiment with this part of the preparation – try things out, keep what you like and change what doesn't work. Again – remember – you won't take all of this action into performance. It is here to help you engage creatively and physically with the text in rehearsal.

Exercise 2

Text	Action	Speaking to?
	I breathe in as I look at all the faces in the audience. I'm trying to decide if I can trust these people. I decide I can. I want them to understand that I am perfectly sane. I know air and (I look up) the sun when I see and feel them.	The audience –although I decide that my best friends, Lisa and Daniel, are in the audience.
This is the air; that is the glorious sun; This pearl she gave me, I do feel't and see't; And though 'tis wonder that enwraps me thus,	*I take out the ring. It is amazing – very expensive and it sparkles in a way that kind of dazzles me.*	
Yet 'tis not madness.	*I think I hear Lisa laughing at me. I put the ring away, look at her and step toward her, to let her know I'm sane.*	

Text	Action	Speaking to?
Where's Antonio, then?	*I think someone here knows where Antonio is – I see my best friend and I know he likes to play practical jokes – but he doesn't have any answers for me.*	I catch Daniel's eye.
I could not find him at the Elephant:	*I also think that some of them think I haven't bothered to look for him.*	Everyone in the audience
Yet there he was; and there I found this credit,	*I set them straight.*	
That he did range the town to seek me out. His counsel now might do me golden service;	*I decide that I will have to charm these people to get any info out of them.*	

Again, this might feel like a lot of thought and action, but for me it is just a good start on this monologue. I like that I have to keep working on seeing familiar faces and making an impression on them. I'll refine and get rid of anything that doesn't serve me once I get to the final rehearsal stage.

Just to recap, when creating your imagined world:

1   Be as detailed and specific as you can.
2   Include physical action, even if it feels like a lot to keep in your head in the early stages. You can always get rid of it later.
3   Always see who you are talking to, and always imagine how they are looking at you, what they're doing, what you think they are feeling/thinking and what you WANT them to feel/think.
4   Always leave your character's feelings out of this preparation.

Conclusion

Between the Introduction and Phase 1, we've done about 13 hours of work now. If you've completed all the exercises and feel like you understand the basics of them, you are ready to go onto the next phase. Try to make sure that you take some time between this section and starting the next. A little unfocused time always helps in the learning process and if you have the chance, once you've finished this section just go for a walk, or go the gym. Don't think in a concentrated way on any of the exercises we've done here, but if you remember things or want to daydream about any of the texts we've covered in the exercises, just let yourself imagine whatever comes to mind.

CHOOSING AND PREPARING THE MONOLOGUE

This section helps you choose and prepare a text for rehearsal, but, in that preparation, you will actually be doing your first rehearsals. The overall time for completing this section is timed as closely as it can be, given that circumstances will vary (some monologues are in prose; some people already have a monologue). Skip 'Choosing the best monologue' if you already have one and skip the meter analysis section if your piece is in prose. But do all of the others, as they form the first block of rehearsal for your final performance.

Choosing the best monologue

0–3 HOURS

You won't always have a choice in this matter – sometimes the monologue is specified in the audition information. Sometimes you are sent a list or given a choice of a few. If you already have a monologue or have been sent something specific to learn, you may be able to skip this step. But if you've been sent a list or are starting from scratch, you will want to match the choice of monologue with your particular strengths.

I am often asked about the ideal length of a monologue or about whether you can cut or edit monologues. If you have been sent a monologue, do it exactly as it is. Don't cut, edit or change anything. And remember that if you're choosing a monologue from a list of six or so, the panel is very likely to know every single word of your monologue well – so make sure you learn it exactly as written. If you haven't been sent a specified list of monologues, you can cut or edit out the lines of others, as long as you retain the sense of the speech and the character's thought process. I generally advise actors to do pieces of twenty lines at least (less than twenty lines will not give you much to work with), and not to exceed forty for audition.

Choosing a monologue is always a challenge and, while there are some general rules about this, I think you should remember that an audition gives you the chance to show a panel who you really are. That might mean that although you are a young woman, you feel very drawn to playing Hamlet. It might mean that you are a thirty-something man, but have great affinity for the strength of Queen Margaret. Only *you* know what really sparks your imagination and gives you the chance to show what you can really do in a strongly imagined world. If you want to choose something very far from your natural casting and know that you can do this better than anything else – do it! Explain your choice briefly to the panel, and be prepared to tell them WHY you chose the piece you did, if asked. I know many actors who worry about doing a piece because it's 'overdone'. I want to try and convince you that this isn't a worry for an audition panel. It's only a worry for the actor.

Most people serving on an audition panel, who have asked for a Shakespeare monologue, don't mind at all if they've heard a piece many times – why else would most drama schools send out a set list? In fact, doing a piece that they know well is very helpful for you. Why? Because all human beings have limited cognitive processing powers. If you come in and do a speech they don't know, they may very well spend much of their time trying to just follow the story of the monologue. An unknown piece requires a significant amount of concentration on the speech itself. This is particularly true when someone comes in and does a clever 'cut and paste' job to make a monologue out of three or four separate speeches. That really sets a challenge for members of the audition panel, because they may begin to wonder exactly where in the play you are and what's going on at that point. But you want ALL of their concentration on YOU. Speaking as someone who auditions people professionally, I would much rather hear a speech I hear often, because that allows me to concentrate on who you are and what you're doing with the speech. That will tell me about your creativity and imagination as an actor.

All of Shakespeare's monologues are good. All of them have depth and poetic ambiguity which allow any actor to truly make the speech their own.

So choose the speech you love. And don't worry about whether it is 'overdone'!

Of course, whichever main piece or pieces you choose, make sure you also have monologues in your portfolio that are from the characters that you are most likely to be cast as. Audition guidance books – or tutors in training situations – routinely advise actors to choose a monologue that 'suits' them. Sometimes this is phrased differently: actors are advised often to choose a monologue spoken by a character that matches their casting type. Overall this is good advice – and certainly some monologues suit some actors better than others – but how is an actor to judge that for themselves? If you don't know Shakespeare's entire canon pretty exhaustively, how are you to know what suits you best? It is a tough job unless you are very familiar with all the works. It seems to me that we need some better tools to deal with the problem of choosing a suitable monologue, so I hope the following section will prove useful for you.

We are going to try to narrow down your possibilities, but remember as we do this that this ISN'T a science. There are no algorithms that will come up with the perfect answer for us, but there are some things we can consider when we are trying to match a monologue to our skill set and 'castability'. We can start with four questions.

Question 1:

What is my favourite kind of writing?
    Romantic/Literary novels
    Thrillers
    Poetry collections

Question 2:

What is the most important thing to me in a book or a film?
    Character
    Writing style/dialogue
    Plot/pace

Question 3:

How would you cast yourself?
    Question 3 is a bit more complicated and needs some thinking time. I want you to concentrate for a moment about how you would cast yourself and I'm going to ask you to do this specifically in terms of *Harry Potter* characters. That probably sounds a bit unusual – but you are more likely to know who Severus Snape is than Philip the Dauphin. The pantheon of *Harry Potter* characters seems to me the most broadly familiar contemporary literary creations of our time and that makes them far more likely to be familiar to those reading this book than the much larger variety of characters that Shakespeare created. Consequently, we are going to use characters from *Harry Potter* to help us think about casting types. If you don't know *Harry Potter* characters at all don't worry – just read the descriptions of each character below and think about what best matches your type or your casting history.

Please don't cast yourself solely on the basis of whether you look or sound exactly like these characters, but rather on whether the description of attributes that follows them seems like you or seems like the kind of roles in which you are often cast.

At the moment, don't worry too much about the chronological age of Shakespeare's characters, except in the cases of the significantly older characters (Lear, Prospero, Margaret in *Richard III*, etc.), but do think in terms of Juvenile, Young Adult and Mature, in terms of the way in which people view you on stage. You could fall into the 'mature' category if you are over thirty and have some gravitas and presence onstage. But you might also fall into that category if you are twenty and keep getting cast as older men or women – some actors just have an inherent weighty presence no matter what their age. You would fall into the 'juvenile' category, if you seem much younger in spirit (and possibly sound). Some actors just have a lighter, more youthful presence on stage, no matter what their age. Young Adult fits most people between eighteen and thirty, but if you are not sure where you fit within these three categories, ask people you trust!

Don't cast yourself the way you WANT to be cast, but the way in which you are most likely to BE cast or have been cast in the past. Remember also, don't rule out casting on the basis of moral choices – some of the best characters are the wicked ones …

What would your casting be among the following? (Choose more than one if appropriate):

Women

Professor McGonagall – *Strong Character: wise, reliable, at times quite harsh, but always good-hearted and loving (even when she hides it). She's not a character you want to cross and she doesn't suffer fools at all. Mature. Good for actors comfortable playing characters who are: decisive, confident and empowered and who tend to intellectualize emotion. Driven by intellectual curiosity and the need to defend the innocent.*

Mrs Weasley – *kind and maternal, but also wise and willing to face up to scary challenges. She's like a mother lion if anyone she loves is threatened and she has a lot of strength to draw upon when a situation gets tough. Young Adult or Mature. Good for actors comfortable playing characters who are: vulnerable, trusting, social, who tend to display emotion freely and are driven by love and care of others.*

Young Hermoine Granger – *Strong all round leading action heroine: wise, compassionate and brave. She has a powerful sense of right and wrong and is instinctively drawn toward goodness. Juvenile or Young Adult. Good for actors comfortable playing characters who are: decisive, open-ended and careful, who display emotion reservedly or freely and are driven by passion, curiosity and desire for justice.*

Older Hermoine Granger – *Strong all round leading action heroine: wise, compassionate, brave. She has all the characteristics of her younger self, but grows more complex and cautious as she matures. Still intellectual, but increasingly more in touch with her emotion and her more loving self as she matures. Juvenile or Young Adult. Good for actors comfortable playing characters who are: decisive, vulnerable, careful, with a tendency to display emotion freely or even extravagantly at times. Driven by curiosity, desire for love and justice.*

Ginny Weasley – *the girl-next-door: dependable, attractive, smart and loyal and definitely 'marriage material'. Stronger than she looks, but allows others to take the lead. Juvenile or Young Adult. Good for actors comfortable playing characters who are: vulnerable, trusting, self-sacrificing, with a tendency to be reserved about displaying emotion in social circumstances. Driven by love and desire.*

Nymphadora Tonks – *an 'outsider' sort of heroine – makes and follows her own rules, but once she decides what is right, she's brave enough to put her heart on the line. A good-hearted person, she's changeable, can be unpredictable, sometimes reckless and impulsive. Juvenile or Young Adult. Good for actors comfortable playing characters who are: confident and vulnerable, with a tendency to display emotion carefully or reservedly in social circumstances. Driven by worldly or spiritual passion and desire.*

Luna Lovegood – *quirky character – strong, wise, off-beat and a bit of a loner. Interested in things that others might not notice. She's brave and willing to put up a fight when necessary, even when no one else agrees with her or sees her point of view. Juvenile or Young Adult. Good for actors comfortable playing characters who are: confident, injured, instinctive and tend to display emotion freely. Driven by passion, curiosity and a desire to control.*

Bellatrix Lestrange – *a warrior: strong, will seem evil and heartless to anyone not affiliated with her 'tribe', beautiful, passionate and dangerous. She's willing to risk anything in her own cause and has no fear of what the world might think of her. She's restless and has a very dark side. Young Adult/Mature. Good for actors comfortable playing characters who are: decisive, confident, entitled, with a tendency to display emotion freely or even extravagantly. Driven by desire and the need to control.*

Rita Skeeter – *sexy, authoritative, mischievous, wily and worldly. She gets what she wants and isn't afraid. Her confidence – even in the worst of circumstances – makes her hard to resist. Young Adult or Mature. Good for actors comfortable playing characters who are: decisive, confident, extroverted, with tendency to display emotion freely or extravagantly. Driven by desire.*

Dolores Umbridge – *despite (possibly motherly) appearance, she has a steely determination to have her way in all things. She is good at hiding her true nature and will do anything in the service of her own cause. Good for actors comfortable playing characters who are: decisive, manipulative, empowered, with varied tendency to display emotion – anywhere from reserved to extravagant. Driven by the need to control or to right injustice.*

Men

Young Harry Potter – *Strong all round leading action hero: rather innocent in the ways of the world, compassionate, brave, but also has a share of humility; he sometimes thinks more of the welfare of others than of himself. Can be obsessed by a single cause or injustice and willing to risk anything to make things right. Juvenile or Young Adult. Good for* *actors comfortable playing characters who are: decisive, independent, vulnerable, injured, with tendency to display emotion freely. Driven by curiosity and desire.*

Older Harry Potter – *Strong all round leading action hero: has grown wiser, remains compassionate and brave, but is increasingly isolated by his own obsessions and is somewhat uncommunicative. A 'complex' hero, who carries the burdens of many others. Juvenile or Young Adult. Good for actors comfortable playing characters who are: decisive, independent, injured, with a tendency to suppress emotion or display reservedly. Driven by a desire for justice.*

Ron Weasley – *somewhat awkward; more a follower than a leader. May have more or less observable personality than typical 'hero' or leading man type, but brave, reliable, fiercely loyal, and willing to serve others. He has a quietly practical nature and is something of an 'everyman' in extraordinary circumstances. Juvenile or Young Adult. Good for actors comfortable playing characters who are: vulnerable, trusting and social. Tendency to display emotion freely, and driven by a need for approval and/or social harmony and justice.*

Lucius Malfoy – *Strong character: quiet, sinister. An arrogant warrior, capable of powerful things. Rebellious and loyal to his own cause at any cost. Has unshakeable conviction, which makes him relatively fearless. But there is a strain of mysterious complexity about him that gives him a sense of torment. Young Adult/Mature. Good for actors comfortable playing characters who are: decisive, entitled and cautious, with a tendency to suppress emotion. Driven by desire for power and a need to control.*

Albus Dumbledore – *wise, strong leader who has commanding authority even in the face of his enemies. Can be whimsical or eccentric and display a wry sense of humour, but has a great store of courage and intellectual curiosity. Mature. Good for actors comfortable playing characters who are: decisive, vulnerable, authoritative, ambiguous, with a tendency to suppress emotion. Driven by desire to right injustice in the world.*

Sirius Black – *the 'troubled' hero, brave and dark and sometimes sinister, fiery, obsessive, but deeply loving. He can be edgy and rebellious, but ultimately craves a just world where he can be accepted for exactly who/what he is. Young Adult or Mature. Good for actors comfortable playing characters who are: vulnerable, instinctive, ambiguous, injured, with tendency to display emotion freely or even extravagantly. Driven by desire to control or to right injustice.*

Severus Snape – *strong character: sarcastic, sometimes unreadable, sinister and ultimately more vulnerable than he looks. He may be a good man with evil tendencies or an evil man with good tendencies. He is extremely complex and his actions are often hard to interpret immediately. Young Adult or Mature. Good for actors comfortable playing characters who are: ambiguous, injured, dangerous, self-entitled and introspective, with a tendency to suppress emotion. Driven by a desire to control or to right an injustice.*

Peter Pettigrew – *strong and very quirky character: colourful, unreliable, may be a joker. Although generally loyal, he is always ultimately self-serving and often jealous of others. Jealousy may drive him to make bad decisions, or just seem rather unapproachable. Young Adult or Mature. Good for actors comfortable playing characters who are: ambiguous, vulnerable, disruptive, with a tendency to display emotion freely. Driven by desire for power, control or approval.*

Cedric Diggory – *intelligent, honest, loyal, brave, trustworthy. A warrior who follows, but not a leader. In different times, he may have been a leader, but he is surrounded* by strong personalities who command. May have a strong romantic streak, but it isn't his most noticeable trait. Juvenile, Young Adult or Mature. Good for actors comfortable playing characters who are: social, trusting and decisive, with tendency to suppress or be cautious about displaying emotion. Driven by passion and the desire to serve.

Neville Longbottom – socially awkward, perhaps a late-blooming hero who has a powerful sense of right and wrong, which gives him courage at times. He is an introverted character who blossoms in dangerous situations. Loyal and self-effacing. Juvenile or Young Adult. Good for actors comfortable playing characters who are: vulnerable, self-sacrificing and trusting, with a tendency to suppress emotion. Driven by a desire for harmony, justice and social order.

Arthur Weasley – hard working, loving, loyal, good-hearted and brave when called upon. Not a leader, but a strong team member. Willing to be self-sacrificing for the right cause. Young Adult or Mature. Good for actors comfortable playing characters who are: vulnerable, social, trusting and self-effacing, who tend to display emotion carefully. Driven by desire to serve.

Hagrid – an awkward outsider, loyal and slightly rebellious at the same time. An earthy humanity and good sense of humour. Utterly loyal to his own cause and can be fiercely loyal to others he has 'adopted' or who have earned his respect. Young Adult or Mature. Good for actors comfortable playing characters who are: vulnerable, social, trusting and extroverted. Tendency to display emotion freely. Driven by desire for approval.

Fred or George Weasley – disruptive, funny, creative character who can't quite be comfortable in traditional roles or settings. These characters find it hard to accept authority and always have their own very unique take on the world. Affable and loyal to those who have earned their respect. Juvenile, Young Adult or Mature. Good for actors comfortable playing characters who are: social, instinctive, decisive and self-entitled, who display emotion freely. Driven by curiosity and passion.

Remus Lupin – dark, loyal, thoughtful and loving, but a seriously tortured soul. Wants desperately to be good, sometimes can't. Although he is fundamentally a good person, he has secrets or obsessions that sometimes drive him off the rails. A fierce warrior who isn't above deception in the pursuit of his own cause. Young Adult or Mature. Good for actors comfortable playing characters who are: vulnerable, injured, and instinctive, who display emotion freely if sometimes rather cautiously. Driven by passion and sense of duty.

Voldemort – evil and openly so. Can be seductive and charming when necessary, but completely untroubled by killing others to gain power. Psychopathic-type villain, who has no concept of the needs or the pain of others. He relishes his own destructive power. Juvenile, Young Adult or Mature. Good for actors comfortable playing characters who are: vulnerable, dangerous and injured, who tend to suppress emotion. Driven by desire for power and need to control.

Gilderoy Lockhart – bright, vain and utterly self-serving. Happy to put himself forward, even knowing his own shortcomings. His vanity can lead him to harm others, simply because he is so self-absorbed, he doesn't see the whole picture. Can be very charming and successful in spite of all that. Juvenile, Young Adult or Mature. Good for actors comfortable playing characters who are: selfish, vulnerable, instinctive and ambiguous, who tend to display emotion freely. Driven by desire or approval.

Dobby – not an elf, of course, but a good-hearted character who is an utterly humble and fiercely loyal servant. Not always able to see the bigger picture and sometimes willing to *deceive in order to serve. Juvenile, Young Adult or Mature. Good for actors comfortable playing characters who are: vulnerable, trusting and self-sacrificing, with a tendency to suppress emotion. Driven by the desire to serve.*

Question 4:

How strong is your imagination?

There are no simple ways to answer Question 4, but there are other questions that will help you think about your imaginative powers. Do you daydream a lot? Do you write fiction or poetry? When you see a beautiful painting or picture, can you easily imagine yourself in it? Can you close your eyes and imagine touching sandpaper or velvet or marble easily? Can you close your eyes and imagine tasting salt or lemon or coffee easily? Can you hear music in your imagination with some detail? Are you strongly empathetic – in other words, when you watch someone laugh do you laugh? When you watch someone cry, do you cry? Do you ever 'take on' someone else's upset or pain?

Think about these questions and be as honest as you can – it will help your choice of audition monologue. Give yourself a score between 1 and 5, with 1 being mostly 'no' answers to the above; 3 being a pretty equal mix of 'yes' and 'no' answers; and 5 being a 'yes' to all of the above.

The information we gain from these four questions can help guide you in choosing a monologue that works well for you.

Here's how to interpret your answers:

Question 1: Narrowing down the field

If you chose Romantic/Literary fiction as your favourite kind of reading, you are more likely to respond strongly to the writing in the Comedies, the Romances or the Tragedies, so may want to look there first in your search for a monologue. You will probably want an even balance between action and description.

If you chose Thrillers as your favourite kind of reading, you are very likely to respond strongly to the straightforward action of most of the Histories. You will probably want a monologue that has a high percentage of action to description.

If you chose poetry, you are likely to respond strongly to the language of plays like *Richard II, Hamlet, As You Like it, Julius Caesar, Romeo and Juliet, Love's Labour's Lost, Henry V, Measure for Measure, Macbeth, King Lear* or *The Tempest*. You will probably be happiest with a monologue that has a higher percentage of description over action.

Comedies	Tragedies	Histories	Romance
All's Well That Ends Well	*Anthony and Cleopatra*	*Henry IV, Part 1*	*Cymbeline*
As You Like it	*Coriolanus*	*Henry IV, Part 2*	*Pericles*
Comedy of Errors	*Hamlet*	*Henry V*	*The Tempest*
Love's Labour's Lost	*Julius*	*Henry VI, Part 1*	*The Winter's Tale*
Measure for Measure	*King Lear*	*Henry VI, Part 2*	
Merry Wives of Windsor	*Macbeth*	*Henry VI, Part 3*	
Merchant of Venice	*Othello*	*Henry VIII*	
Midsummer Night's Dream	*Romeo and Juliet*	*King John*	
Much Ado About Nothing	*Timon of Athens*	*Richard II*	
Taming of the Shrew	*Titus Andronicus*	*Richard III*	
Troilus and Cressida			
Twelfth Night			
Two Gentlemen of Verona			

Question 2: Matching your literary/film preferences to a monologue

If you chose Character, it is very likely that you will respond strongly to the more psychologically based monologues or monologues that have a bit of exploration of character in them. Look for soliloquies that describe the thoughts of characters and the psychological challenges in complex situations. (Hamlet's, Macbeth's, Richard II's or Juliet's monologues are good examples of this.)

If you chose writing style/dialogue, it is very likely that you will respond strongly to monologues that make much of language – either in wit, metaphor or sheer brilliance of writing. (Berowne's, Benedict's or Rosalind's monologues are a good example of this.)

If you chose plot/pace, it is very likely that you will respond strongly to monologues that have a very action-based, plot-driven feel. (Most monologues in the History plays are a good example of this.)

Question 3: Matching your casting type to a monologue

You will find full monologue lists, based on your casting choices at the end of the book, Appendix A. These lists are designed to help you narrow down your choices, but of course they aren't meant to suggest that Shakespeare's characters are exact matches to the characters found in the *Harry Potter* series – it is just a good way to group types of characters/monologues and to help you try to see what monologues might suit your casting type. *Harry Potter* characters are far from an exact match to Shakespeare's characters, but they do share some traits or characteristics.

Question 4: Matching the strength of your imagination to a monologue

Overall, monologues that represent moments of peak, personal crisis or disintegration are probably best avoided in audition. Most actors who have played Margaret, Cleopatra or Hamlet in production will tell you that it takes five acts of concentrated imagination to produce the depth of real anguish that some of their later monologues require. An audition room isn't likely to provide a context that supports such work.

Still, many of Shakespeare's monologues require much of the actor in terms of emotional connection and that in turn demands powerful imaginative skill.

You might be well advised to select a monologue depending on how you answered the questions about the strength of your imagination:

- If you are in the '1' or '2' territory, avoid anything overtly emotional. Stick to monologues that have one or more very direct actions and a very clear, perhaps urgent context.

- If you are in the '3' territory, avoid monologues that have extreme emotional contexts. You can certainly choose more delicate, nuanced and deeply felt monologues, however, and you have a pretty wide range of choices.

- If you are in the '4' or '5' territory, you are probably going to enjoy monologues that have very powerful circumstances – life and death sort of situations. You are likely to be drawn to the most extreme, but remember that these can be very taxing unless you are an actor with enough skill and experience to relish the difficulty of them and don't feel daunted by the challenge of making bold emotional choices on your own in an audition room.

I think it is important to remember at this point that audition <u>panels are not interested in whether an actor can cry on demand or shout with rage on cue</u> – trust me, they've seen quite a lot of that. What they are looking for is a strength of imagination that can give the world of your monologue detail and clarity. They are looking for a complex and active thought process, and they are looking for range and passion in the use of language.

How the 'bare bones' affects your choice

Once you've found a couple of monologues you like, do a quick bare bones exercise on your two or three favourites. You may have any number of possibilities, but it is worth doing a rough bare bones analysis on all of them. That analysis will help you gauge the balance of action to description. Once you know that, you can try to match it with your preferences.

On the whole (and this is only a *general* rule), I would advise that for an audition monologue, you keep the description to at least an even balance (50 per cent action, 50 per cent description). This is because an audition situation is unique, and you will be performing under pressure. At these moments we need all the tools we can get, and – as we'll be seeing – the more we can externalize what we are doing, the more likely we are to keep nerves under control and text in our command. Of course we know that there are times when we MUST do a requested monologue, and that requires different strategies. But when we have the choice, a fairly even balance of action to description (at the very least) is good. More action than description is even better. Finally, no matter where your reflection on these questions lead you, make sure that whatever you choose inspires you in terms of the imagined world in which the monologue is set. If you've chosen a monologue that you like, but can't imagine anything happening around it or have anyone to talk to, I would counsel you to choose another. The more you can bring an imagined world to life around your speech, the better your performance is going to be.

Read through the whole process first

1 HOUR

In order to get the absolute best out of this process, I ask you to follow this process as closely as you can. What we are aiming to do here is to engage with the text in ways that will not only help us to unleash our creative responses, but also help us to remember both words and action in a way that feels easy and not forced, or stressful.

It is probably going to feel very different from any preparation you've done before. Although we are preparing the text for rehearsal, the preparation itself IS part of your rehearsal. You will understand that better once you get started. There are the two rules:

1   **Resist the urge to return to your old ways, and try to trust me on this process**. Don't do any of your 'usual' prep things. Don't throw yourself into the monologue emotionally, don't do lots of emotional performances in your bedroom, don't record yourself and don't try to memorize anything. Just follow these steps exactly as they're laid out. I think you will find that it radically improves both the enjoyment you get from the experience, but because you will engage with the text in so many ways, you will feel more confident in performance.

2   **There's absolutely no substitute for hard work in this preparation.** That doesn't mean it has to take forever – in fact, if you will follow the time guidelines, you will surprised at how much more secure and confident you feel, in probably less time than you were spending in your old, habitual process. In each section I've put an estimate of the time you will need to complete. It is impossible to say exactly how much time you will need, because that depends on the complexity of the speech you've chosen, whether it is in verse or not, and how quickly you read. So I've tried to also include a number of

times that you should do a particular exercise. Do NOT do less than the indicated number. You can, of course, do more if you have the time, but the number of repetitions of an exercise that I've indicated is the least that you will need to do in order to feel fully prepared. Read the process all the way through before you do anything, so that you can plan your preparation time well in advance. This is especially important if you are under very tight time constraint.

It will take you about an hour to read this whole section first before you start preparing your own monologue. When you finish you will understand the preparation process and how it is structured. Then you can go back and prepare your monologue in the order laid out below.

In the process descriptions below, I've chosen an example monologue that many would consider tough for audition, because it is rather long, and there are really only two actions in it: Juliet says goodbye to her mother and her nurse, and then she takes the drug given to her by the Friar. But she spends some forty-odd lines getting from action 1 to action 2. Consequently, it is a mostly descriptive monologue: she describes every misgiving, every doubt, every fear she has about the plan, about the drug, about the friar and about the terror of waking up in the tomb.

I'll use this monologue to demonstrate every step in this preparation phase and, once you've read through the demonstrations, you can plan how you'll do each section with your chosen monologue in your own allotted time. If you have two weeks, you'll be in great shape. If you have only one week, you'll need to plot these times into your calendar very carefully. When you've finished reading through, you are ready to get started on the work.

Get to know the context of the monologue

1–3 HOURS

If you know the play that your monologue is taken from, you may not need more than an hour. But make sure that you brush up your memory of the scene that the monologue occurs in – especially what happens in the few pages before you speak. Also, make sure that you've looked up every word and that you understand everything in the text. A great site for helping with this is www.shakespeareswords. com. It may be heresy, but I don't always expect that actors will have read an entire play when they do a monologue – especially if they're under time pressure. This is because reading Shakespeare's plays can be very confusing if you are new to them. At the very least, however, you should read a good synopsis and perhaps get a character breakdown – www.PlayShakespeare.com is an excellent site for doing both these things. If you can, view the act that your monologue is taken from (YouTube, or libraries are excellent sources for this).

Be very careful about using sources like No Fear Shakespeare, because in their desire to translate Shakespeare's language into contemporary idiom, they very often collapse ambiguity and over-simplify things in a way that is severely limiting for an actor. If you are absolutely stumped by a phrase, consult notes in a Norton or Arden edition – they're available everywhere and you should be able to work everything out from these sources. If you are not under severe time pressure, do read or watch a video of the play – there are a lot of excellent versions out there and most are inexpensive. Of course, seeing the play live might prove even better, but it is not always possible.

Analyzing structure

3 HOURS

At this point you may have a bare bone version of your chosen monologue – but if you don't, do that here. A maximum time is 3 hours – many people can do both of these exercises in less time, but you want to find good, strong images, so may need the maximum time given.

As you see here, I've put the monologue on one side of the paper and the bare bones on the other. You can see that in the second half, this monologue has a higher percentage of description over action and, therefore, might not play to your strengths. But the first half is fairly active.

Text	Bare bones
Farewell! God knows when we shall meet again.	*Farewell! God knows when we shall meet*
I have a (faint cold) fear thrills through my veins,	*I have a fear thrills through my veins*
That (almost) freezes up (the heat of) life:	*That freezes up life*
I'll call them back (again) to comfort me:	*I'll call them back to comfort me*
Nurse! What should she do here?	*Nurse! What should she do here?*
(My dismal scene) I (needs) must act alone.	*I must act alone*
Come, vial.	*Come vial*
What if this mixture do not work (at all)?	*What if this mixture do not work?*
Shall I be married (then) to-morrow (morning)?	*Shall I be married tomorrow?*
No, (no:) this shall forbid it: lie thou there.	*No –this [dagger] shall forbid. Lie thou there*
Laying down her dagger	
What if it be a poison, which the friar (Subtly) hath minister'd (to have me dead,)	*What if it be a poison which the friar Hath minister'd*
Lest in this marriage he should be dishonour'd,	*Lest he be dishonour'd*
Because he married me before to Romeo?	*Because he married me before to Romeo?*
I fear it is: and yet, (methinks,) it should not,	*I fear it is: and yet, it should not [be]*
For he hath (still) been tried a holy man.	*For he hath been tried a holy man.*
How if, when (I am) laid into the tomb,	*How if, when laid into the tomb*
I wake before the time that Romeo	*I wake before the time that Romeo*
Come to redeem me? (there's a fearful point!)	*Come to redeem me?*

Text	Bare bones
Shall I (not, then,) be stifled in the vault,	*Shall I be stifled in the vault*
(To) whose (foul) mouth no healthsome air breathes (in,)	*Whose mouth no healthsome air breathes*
And there die strangled (ere my Romeo comes)?	*And there die strangled?*
Or, if I live, is it not (very) like,	*If I live, is it not like*
(The horrible conceit of death and night,	
Together with) the terror of the place,–	*The terror of the place*
(As in a vault, an ancient receptacle,)	
Where, (for these many hundred years,) the bones	*Where the bones*
Of (all) my (buried) ancestors are packed:	*of my ancestors are packed*
Where (bloody) Tybalt,(yet but green in earth),	*Where Tybalt*
Lies festering (in his shroud;) where(, as they say,	*lies festering, where*
At some hours in the night) spirits resort;–	*Spirits resort;*
(Alack, alack, is it not like that I,	*Is it not like that I*
So early waking, what with loathsome smells,	*so early waking, what with loathsome smells*
And shrieks (like mandrakes' torn out of the earth,	*And shrieks*
That living mortals, hearing them, run mad:–	
O, if I wake,) shall I not be distraught,	*Shall I not be distraught,*
Environed with (all these hideous) fears?	*Environed with fears?*
And (madly) play with (my) forefather's joints?	*And play with forefather's joints?*
And pluck (the mangled) Tybalt from his shroud?	*And pluck Tybalt from his shroud?*
And, in this rage, (with some great kinsman's bone,	*And, in this rage,*
As with a club,) dash out my (desperate) brains?	*Dash out my brains?*
(O,) look! (methinks) I see my cousin's ghost	*Look! I see my cousin's ghost*
Seeking out Romeo, (that did spit his body	*Seeking out Romeo*
Upon a rapier's point:) stay, Tybalt(, stay)!	*Stay, Tybalt!*
Romeo, I come! (this do) I drink to thee.	*Romeo I come. I drink to thee.*

Once you've created your own bare bones monologue, print it off and put it into a working notebook – this is the book you will be using when we get to the rehearsal phase. Read it through at least five times, refining as you go.

Now answer the questions that we looked at in Phase 1 after each bare bones analysis. Here are my example answers for the Juliet monologue:

- *What is the (Juliet's) main action?*
  Juliet's main action is to allay her fears and find the courage to drink the Friar's mixture.

- *What is the balance of action to descriptive/repetitive language here?*
  About 65/35

- *What do you make of the parenthetical words and phrases here? Any strong imagery or metaphors? Do these tell you anything about (Juliet) or her world?*
  In terms of the parenthetical language, we don't learn much about Juliet's world, apart from the fact that her ancestor's bones are preserved in a vault – that tells you much about her status. But beyond that, the most important thing we learn is just how extreme her situation is. The strongest imagery is all to do with the vault and the things she's frightened of. 'Dismal', 'fearful', 'horrible', 'bloody', 'hideous', 'mangled', 'desperate' are much of what we find in the parenthetical phrases, which tells you just where her heart and mind are centred during this speech. But perhaps more importantly, this analysis has made me realize that there aren't lengthy parenthetical sections, which makes this speech surprisingly active – despite its descriptive nature. That's because it is structured as a series of questions and questions are always active. If you go back to look at the 'bare bones' side of the speech above it is much easier to see this – there are ten questions in total. Quite a lot for one monologue!

After reading your bare bones version through a few times, you will probably have a sense of its units or sections. Most actors are familiar with the idea of units in a speech or scene, but if you aren't, a unit is basically a section of thought or action. A new unit begins with a new thought or a new action. I've spent some time with the Juliet monologue now and I've decided that there are six main units. Everyone will do this kind of 'uniting' differently – that's not important. The only important thing is that you resist the urge to create too many. The usual number of units in a monologue is four to six and that's about what you can easily hold in your working memory. Try to keep your 'units' to between four and six. Here are my six sample units and with each unit, you will see that I have found a picture that connects me to what is happening:

UNIT 1: Becoming aware of being alone and of the dangerous thing I'm about to do:

Farewell! God knows when we shall meet again.
I have a faint cold fear thrills through my veins,
That almost freezes up the heat of life:
I'll call them back again to comfort me:
Nurse! What should she do here?
My dismal scene I needs must act alone.
Come, vial.
What if this mixture do not work at all?
Shall I be married then to-morrow morning?
No, no: this shall forbid it: lie thou there.

UNIT 2: 'Seeing' the Friar in mind and doubting him, then trusting him:

What if it be a poison, which the friar
Subtly hath minister'd to have me dead,
Lest in this marriage he should be dishonour'd,
Because he married me before to Romeo?
I fear it is: and yet, methinks, it should not,
For he hath still been tried a holy man.

UNIT 3: *Thinking about waking up alone in the vault, and then dying before Romeo arrives:*

How if, when I am laid into the tomb,
I wake before the time that Romeo
Come to redeem me? there's a fearful point!
Shall I not, then, be stifled in the vault,
To whose foul mouth no healthsome air breathes in,
And there die strangled ere my Romeo comes?

UNIT 4: *Getting very scared by old graves, bones, ghosts and Tybalt:*

Or, if I live, is it not very like,
The horrible conceit of death and night,
Together with the terror of the place, –
As in a vault, an ancient receptacle,
Where, for these many hundred years, the bones
Of all my buried ancestors are packed:
Where bloody Tybalt, yet but green in earth,
Lies festering in his shroud; where, as they say,
At some hours in the night spirits resort; –

UNIT 5: *Letting my imaginary fears drive me into imagining that I might kill myself:*

Alack, alack, is it not like that I,
So early waking, what with loathsome smells,
And shrieks like mandrakes' torn out of the earth,

That living mortals, hearing them, run mad: –
O, if I wake, shall I not be distraught,
Environed with all these hideous fears?
And madly play with my forefather's joints?
And pluck the mangled Tybalt from his shroud?
And, in this rage, with some great kinsman's bone,
As with a club, dash out my desperate brains?

UNIT 6: Letting Tybalt's ghost help me make up my mind:

O, look! methinks I see my cousin's ghost
Seeking out Romeo, that did spit his body
Upon a rapier's point: stay, Tybalt, stay!
Romeo, I come! this do I drink to thee.

This sectioning helps me to distinguish what is, basically, a long descriptive passage full of questions and also will eventually make the whole monologue much easier to learn. You don't want TOO many sections, but you want enough to hold the speech in your head. Now that you have these units and pictures (or drawings) to go with each one, print them off and put them into your 'working notebook'.

You can also just print off a visual sequence of the pictures without text:

While you are doing this part of the process, spend time finding pictures that really stay with you – something that connects with you on a personal level and that will remind you of your summary of each unit. The fifth image above makes me think of dashing my brains out with 'some great kinsman's bone' – it gives me a strong memory link. The internet has made this search easy now, so dig in and find the best, most memorable images you can.

I've used a lot of concentration now, so I want to lean back, and just look at my pictures and take a 5-minute break. While I do I'm just going to add any little details to them that I can. For example – I might add a hug to my nurse or see the friar handing me the vial of poison. I might add a few more images, like a vault. I might try to see the ghostly image handing me a drink. I'm just going to let go and let my imagination work with these pictures. I'm going to imagine myself moving from picture to picture.

At this point, you should feel as if you have a strong sense of the structure of monologue. Resist trying to do anything more than we've outlined here for this very first session. If you can, take a break now. Go walking or do something else entirely. Every now and then, just reflect on the six pictures and add any other details you want. Don't do anything except bring the pictures into your mind from time to time.

SUMMARY

1   Create a bare bones version of the monologue.

2   Answer three questions: (a) What is the main action? (b) What is
    the balance of action to description/repetition? (3) What do you
    make of the parenthetical language? Are there any strong images or
    metaphors? Do these tell you anything about the character and the
    world of the character?

3   Break the monologue into units.

4   Find pictures for each unit.

5   Put all this into your working notebook.

6   Relax and clear your mind, but let pictures float up into
    consciousness if they do.

Analyzing rhythm

1 HOUR

You will need a clean print of the text for this. This time you are just going to go through everything in the speech, analyze rhythm and concentrate on what the rhythm might tell us. My example looks like this:

Text	Meter
Farewell! God knows when we shall meet again.	even
I have a faint cold fear thrills through my veins,	even
That almost freezes up the heat of life:	even
I'll call them back again to comfort me:	even
Nurse! What should she do here?	partial line – *as if stopping in her tracks?*
My dismal scene I needs must act alone.	even
Come, vial.	partial line – *as if seeing for the first time?*
What if this mixture do not work at all?	even
Shall I be married then to-morrow morning?	feminine ending
No, no: this shall forbid it: lie thou there.	even
Laying down her dagger	
What if it be a poison, which the friar	even *(elide 'fryr')*
Subtly hath minister'd to have me dead,	even – *but 'subt-ly' is rocky so even out stresses*
Lest in this marriage he should be dishonour'd,	feminine ending
Because he married me before to Romeo?	feminine ending
I fear it is: and yet, methinks, it* should not,	feminine, *but I can elide: me'thinks't should not' – that makes it even*
For he hath still been tried a holy man.	*even*
How if, when I am laid into the tomb,	even
I wake before the time that Romeo	even
Come to redeem me? there's a fearful point!	even – *but 'Come to' is rocky, so even out stresses*

Shall I not, then, be stifled in the vault,	even
To whose foul mouth no healthsome air breathes in,	even
And there die strangled ere my Romeo comes?	even (if you elide 'Rom-yo')
Or, if I live, is it not very like,	even
The horrible conceit of death and night,	even
Together with the terror of the place,–	even
As in a vault, an ancient receptacle,	rocky- *as if thinking about how old vault is?*
Where, for these many hundred years, the bones	even
Of all my buried ancestors are packed:	even
Where bloody Tybalt, yet but green in earth,	even
Lies festering in his shroud; where, as they say,	*even – but elide 'fest'ring'*
At some hours in the night spirits resort;–	*even – but 'spi-**rits**' is rocky so even out stresses*
Alack, alack, is it not like that I,	even
So early waking, what with loathsome smells,	even
And shrieks like mandrakes' torn out of the earth,	even
That living mortals, hearing them, run mad:–	even
O, if I wake, shall I not be distraught,	even
Environed with all these hideous fears?	*even (add –'ed': en-**vi**-ron-**ed** & elide 'hid'ous')*
And madly play with my forefather's joints?	even
And pluck the mangled Tybalt from his shroud?	even
And, in this rage, with some great kinsman's bone,	even
As with a club, dash out my desperate brains?	*even – elide 'desp'rate'*
O, look! methinks I see my cousin's ghost	even
Seeking out Romeo, that did spit his body	*feminine – even out stress on 'seeking' & elide 'ro-myo'*
Upon a rapier's point: stay, Tybalt, stay!	even
Romeo, I come! this do I drink to thee.	*even – elide 'Rom'yo'*

It is a surprisingly even monologue, given the emotional weight of the piece – this is a good thing, as all that even rhythm will help with memorization. Remember that in rocky lines – especially when they 'rock' towards the front (like 'Subtly' and 'Seeking' above), just even out the stresses until you feel the line fall into a natural rhythm again.

Once you've done the meter analysis like this on your monologue, print it out and add it to your working notebook. You should have some time left, so practice the meter out loud ten times in an exaggerated way. REMEMBER THIS IS NOT AN ACTING EXERCISE.

It is a sound and rhythm exercise, so leave your emotion out of this completely at this point. You can, however, try to make the meaning of the lines clear. As you go through the first three times, check your analysis – you might find more things out about the rhythm and you may discover places where you are not quite sure how the meter works. Just do your best to see if/how you can make any sense of the 'rocky' lines. Make sure you have written in reasons (as I have above) for rhythm changes – even if you are only guessing at this point.

After you've done readings out loud, do three more. This time, involve yourself physically: clap your hands on the stresses; walk around and step harder on stresses; punch a pillow on the stresses; punch like a boxer on the stresses – anything that gets you moving.

In your last two repetitions, make the stresses as exaggerated as you can, while delivering the monologue to an imaginary group of children – and either terrify them or make them laugh. Everything MUST be exaggerated here, stresses, sounds of words (choose the really descriptive words and make something of them!). Act out any physical things described in the speech. Again – this is not about making an emotional connection to the speech – this is about making children either giggly or terrified.

Now you have gone through this eight times very mechanically and clearly, assess whether you still think you have the units right in the monologue. I decided that I did have them right, but noticed some interesting patterns. Pattern is in our next session.

This has been a quick, but very concentrated session. So, it's time to relax now. Just lean back and go through your picture sequence again. You will probably still feel the pulse of the iambic pentameter rhythm in your mind/body – that's fine, just enjoy feeling that pulse. It is like a heartbeat. Tonight, before you go to sleep, run through your unit picture sequence. Also, before you go to sleep, if any of the text comes back to you in the strong rhythm, just let it come. Don't try to remember, just enjoy the text if you find that you do.

SUMMARY

1   Analyze meter and if there are any 'rocky' lines, imagine what might be the reason for that. Even out stresses when they rock and make sure that the sound makes sense as you read.

2   Read out loud three times, exaggerating the meter and checking sound/analysis as you go to make sure you have it right.

3   Read out loud three times, while physicalizing the meter.

4   Read out loud two times to an imaginary group of children – exaggerate the meter and either terrify or make the children laugh.

5   Relax and clear your mind.

Finding language patterns

1 HOUR

Patterns help us in the early stages of learning. They help to cluster together certain ideas, and to make connections in the bigger picture of the piece. Some monologues are so dominated by the patterns Shakespeare created in them that if the actor does nothing more than emphasize the patterns of the speech, they will probably be well on their way to creating a strong acting performance. This brief passage from *Richard II* demonstrates that idea clearly. Here, in a short passage, Richard repeats his title, 'king', four times in the first four lines, to remind his usurpers exactly who he is. He cleverly repeats 'must' when he says 'king' because he wants to make it clear that kings should never be in the position where they 'must' do *anything*. So, he might be opposing the idea of a 'king' with the idea of a person who 'must obey' – certainly they SHOULD be opposites. He also opposes 'must' with 'shall'. You could try reading this speech while emphasizing either one of these oppositions. When you work on oppositions in a speech, just imagine that you are thinking 'I have THIS on the one hand, and THAT on the other'. Try the first four lines of this speech out loud, opposing the word 'must' against the word 'king':

> What **must** the **king** do now? **Must** he submit?
> The **king** shall do it: **must** he be deposed?
> The **king** shall be contented: **must** he lose
> The name of **king**? O' God's name, let it go:

Now try those four lines and very consciously oppose the word 'must' with the word 'shall':

> What **must** the king do now? **Must** he submit?
> The king **shall** do it: **must** he be deposed?
> The king **shall** be contented: **must** he lose
> The name of king? O' God's name, let it go:

You'll probably get a strong feeling about what Richard is doing here and, by working the two different oppositions, you'll probably feel a subtle difference in the way Richard is using language to shame the rebels. He goes on to use a series of oppositions to illustrate the extremity of the crime of dethroning an anointed king, and suggests that the enormity of it all will send him to his grave:

I'll **g**ive my *jewels* for a set of *beads*, *[jewels vs beads]*
My **g**orgeous *palace* for a *hermitage,* *[palace vs hermitage]*
My **g**ay *apparel* for an *almsman's gown*, *[gay apparel vs almsman's gown]*
My *figured* **g**oblets for a *dish of wood*, *[figured goblets vs dish of wood]*
My **s**ceptre for a palmer's walking **s**taff, *[sceptre vs staff]*
My **s**ubjects for a pair of carved **s**aints, *[subjects vs saints]*
And my *large kingdom* for a **little** *grave*, *[large kingdom v. little grave]*
A **little little** grave, an obscure grave

This is a great piece for looking at patterns like repetition, oppositions and alliteration.

The repeated use of sounds (the hard 'g' of 'give', 'gorgeous', 'gay', 'gown', 'goblets', 'grave') and the 'little, little, little' repetition at the end, add to an incredibly powerful combination of sounds and ideas that make Richard's position clear, and Bolingbroke's crime extraordinary. If you read the passage through, doing nothing more than emphasizing the repetitions, oppositions and alliterations, Richard's actions will be very clear to the listener.

But patterns don't simply help you clarify ideas and structure, they can be helpful for remembering ideas and the structure of a piece. When I was working on 'uniting' my Juliet piece I noticed that there are four stages of her fear:

- The first is that she is being tricked by the friar into drinking poison.

- The second is of being strangled/stifled in an airless vault before Romeo comes.

- The third fear is of seeing ghosts and bones of her dead ancestors arising.

- The fourth fear is that the smells and shrieks will make her crazy and lead her to 'dash out her brains'.

That pattern will help me to distinguish the long descriptive passages and will eventually make this speech much easier to learn.

The patterns in Juliet's speech aren't as clear as the ones in the *Richard II* speech above – but that makes it all the more important that I find whatever repetitions, oppositions, themes or alliterations that I can. Patterns help to 'cement' the structure in our heads. The main patterns to look for are:

- Repetitions
- Oppositions
- Alliteration
- Other similar sounds or ideas

After reading through out loud many times in the last session, I noticed these repeated phrases:

- What if, What if, How if, Or if
- I wake, So early waking, O if I wake
- Is it not very like, Alack, is it not like
- Bloody Tybalt, mangled Tybalt, stay Tybalt

These alliterations in Unit 4:

- Bones, buried, bloody

These alliterations in Unit 5:

- Mandrakes, mortals, mad

These one-syllable verbs in Unit 5:

- Play, pluck, dash

Any pattern we can find helps us later when we are retrieving the text, so I'm just going to plot these patterns in bold on the monologue. You can do this on computer if you have a colour printer, but it is much better to go 'old school' and just do this with marker pens. Colour is a strong visual memory aid. I'm going to lay this out in our usual, two-column page, but as I can't use colour here, I just have to use different fonts, circles and underlines to lay out the patterns.

Once you've marked up all your patterns, put the sheet into your working notebook.

Farewell! God knows when we shall meet again.
I have a faint cold fear thrills through my veins,
That almost freezes up the heat of life:
I'll call them back again to comfort me:
Nurse! What should she do here?
My dismal scene I needs must act alone.
Come, vial.
What if this mixture do not work at all?
Shall I be married then to-morrow morning?
No, no: this shall forbid it: lie thou there.

What if it be a poison, which the friar
Subtly hath minister'd to have me dead,
Lest in this marriage he should be dishonour'd,
Because he married me before to Romeo?
I fear (it is): and yet, methinks, (it should not),
For he hath still been tried a holy man.
How if, when I am laid into the tomb,
I wake before the time that Romeo
Come to redeem me? there's a fearful point!
Shall I not, then, be stifled in the vault,
To whose (foul mouth) no (healthsome air) breathes in,
And there (die) strangled ere my Romeo comes?
Or, if I (live), *is it not very like,*
The horrible conceit of death and night,
Together with the terror of the place,–
As in a vault, an ancient receptacle,
Where, for these many hundred years, the **BONES**
Of all my **BURIED** ancestors are packed:
Where BLOODY TYBALT, yet but green in earth,
Lies festering in his shroud; **where,** as they say,
At some hours in the night spirits resort;–
Alack, alack, *is it not like* that I,
So early waking, what with loathsome smells,
And shrieks like **MANDRAKES'** torn out of the earth,
That living **MORTALS,** hearing them, run **MAD:–**
O, if I wake, shall I not be distraught,
Environed with all these hideous fears?
And madly **PLAY** with my forefather's joints?
And **PLUCK** the MANGLED TYBALT from his shroud?
And, in this rage, with some great kinsman's bone,
As with a club, **DASH** out my desperate brains?
O, look! methinks I see my cousin's ghost
Seeking out Romeo, that did spit his body
Upon a rapier's point: STAY, TYBALT, stay!
Romeo, I come! this do I drink to thee.

Fears:

The friar is trying to kill me

I'll die before Romeo comes

Ghosts of ancestors & other spirits

Hideous place will drive me to kill myself

Repeated phrases:

- **What if, What if, How if, Or if**

- *I wake, So early waking, O if I wake*

- ***WHERE, WHERE, WHERE***

- **Is it not very like, Alack, is it not like**

- BLOODY TYBALT, MANGLED TYBALT, STAY TYBALT

Oppositions:
(it is) v. (it should not)
(foul mouth) v. (healthsome air)
(die) v. (live)

These alliterations in unit 4:

- **BONES, BURIED, BLOODY**

These alliterations in unit 5:

- **MANDRAKES, MORTALS, MAD**

These 1-syllable verbs in unit 5:

- **PLAY, PLUCK, DASH**

Even in this sparsely patterned monologue, you can see something interesting: the patterns or repetitions, alliterations, etc. occur mostly in the last third of the monologue, when her imagination is running at its wildest.

Before you leave this exercise, just go through each pattern in your monologue, reading them aloud five times. Read the whole line, rather than just a word or two, and stress all the pattern words quite strongly – even as you read the rest of the line in strong iambic meter. As you do this, just imagine seeing what you are talking about. Don't glaze over or just repeat the text without seeing an image of what you are describing.

Once you've finished this, relax. Just close your eyes and try to clear your mind. Let any images that float up, just float up!

SUMMARY

1   Look for:
  - **Repetitions**
  - **Oppositions**
  - **Alliteration**
  - **Other similar sounds or ideas.**
2   Mark these up in various colours on a clean copy of the text.
3   Put this into your working notebook.
4   Relax, and clear your mind.

How to draw a monologue

3 HOURS

I know how strange this sounds, but there is a real purpose to it. It isn't easy to draw a monologue, but be creative. Sometimes you only have to draw something that SOUNDS like a word. And, the more absurd the drawing, the better it will serve its purpose. Essentially, drawing the monologue and learning it while in rehearsal is designed to take the place completely of sitting in your bedroom learning by rote memorization. In order for you to benefit fully from this method, it is important that you give up trying to memorize lines in whatever method you have used in the past.

So how do you draw a monologue? Well, basically, any way you CAN. Here is an example of a student's drawing of Julia's first monologue in *Two Gentlemen of Verona*:

This is an excerpt from my drawing of one of Mark Antony's speeches in *Julius Caesar*:

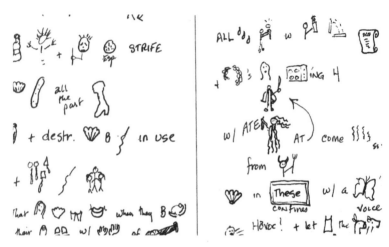

Clearly, it is not going to be hanging in the National Gallery anytime soon. But the truth is, the sillier your image, the better your memory of it will be. As you can see, I do write in some words, but the majority of the speech is rendered in silly little stick men and strange objects that remind me of a word. However you do it, you must make sure that when you look at it, you know exactly what every little drawing means. By its nature, it will probably only have meaning for you – if you look at my drawing above, there may be some things you can decipher, but there will be many things you can't. Still – when I look at it, every little image makes sense.

You might want to draw a little picture that suggests the meaning of a phrase. I did this with the phrase 'in these confines', in which I'm just imagining a word trapped within a confining space.

Or you might want to draw something that is similar to the word you are depicting, but is actually another thing entirely. I did that with 'a monarch', which is picture of a 'monarch' butterfly. It is just an association that makes sense to me and it is so memorable when I look at it. Make the drawings personal; make them mean something; be creative and try to enjoy it. It takes a little time, but this is going to become an important rehearsal tool, so do it as well as you can.[1]

Short common words (and, then, that, for, if, what, etc.) are particularly tough, which is why I tend to write them out, or else find a standard visual that always reminds me of that short word.

However you do it, this is the ONLY script you will use once you've done it. DON'T go back to the written word now, except to check for accuracy the first few times you go through the drawing. When you've finished it, check it carefully against the text and then put it in your working notebook, as this will become your working script in rehearsal.

---

[1] For those of you who are wondering what the point of this is, there is good research to show the relationship between drawing and memory. But, basically, visualization significantly aids the process of remembering or, in the words of science, 'visuospatial attentional orienting optimizes encoding and maintenance in visual short term memory in adults'. Now – aren't you glad you went into the arts?

Depending on how frustrating or pleasurable you find this exercise, you should expect to spend 2–3 hours, but don't do this all at once if you find this hard going. Do as much as you can in an hour and then come back to it later. If you need 2 two-hour sessions to do this, don't worry – that is time well spent. You are about to find out how hard it is to draw a monologue, but don't give up! For Juliet's forty-line monologue, I felt I had to do it in two sessions – I did an hour-and-a-half on one day and an hour-and-a-half on the next. Because it is so important to create unique visuals (this makes it more likely you will retain them), it can be slow going, however.

You will find this easiest if you have some simple symbols that can indicate words like 'and', 'me', 'he', etc. Sometimes you won't be able to draw a word, so write it out, but write it in a funny or memorable way.

Once you've done ten lines worth of drawing, go back through it carefully. Fix anything that confuses you and, if any of your images are too hard to read, keep them, but write the word in under them. Don't try to remember anything at this point, don't ACT, just read through and make sure that everything matches the meter and the text exactly as it is.

Once you are sure the drawing is absolutely correct, go through it six times:

1   The first three times just 'read' through and enjoy the drawings. Make sure you understand everything and that it is all correct (if you can, get someone to hold your monologue and correct you if you go wrong anywhere when you are reading the 'picture' monologue).

2   The second three times, do it in mechanical, exaggerated meter. Because you are 'reading' pictures, you will find this easiest if you pound on the desk or tap your foot quite hard as you do it. Fix anything that needs fixing and enjoy the look of the drawings you've made – remember the sillier the drawing, the more it stays with you. On the sixth read through, you should be able to read it though in as word-perfect a style as you can read the actual text.

You've probably spent about 3 hours now, so it is time to relax. Sit back. Put the text and the drawing away. Close your eyes and concentrate on your breathing. Let any images that rise up in your mind just be there, but don't try to connect anything, unless your mind actually WANTS to connect things. Don't force anything, and *don't try to remember*.

Before you go to bed, read through your drawing at least five times. However, you've scheduled your time for completing your full audition preparation (2 hours a day for seven days? 3 hours a day for five days?), make sure you go through your drawing every night before you go to sleep and remember to keep trying to just follow it along in meter without being tempted to memorize or act out anything. We are still in 'technical mode' and we don't want emotion clouding things right now.

SUMMARY

1   Draw the monologue, checking for accuracy as you go.
2   Read the drawing three times, continuing to check for accuracy and amend in any place where you weren't sure of the drawing.
3   Read the drawing three times, trying to add the meter in an exaggerated way.
4   Put the drawing into your working notebook.
5   Relax and clear your mind.
6   Review the drawing every night before you go to sleep.

Create the imagined world of the speech

$$3$$
$$\textbf{HOURS}$$

This exercise takes focus, so make sure you are taking breaks every 20–30 minutes and just allowing your mind to drift before you go back into the focused mode of work. At this point we've identified the main action/s of the speech, so the work at hand now is all about creating the imagined conditions wherein your action/s is/are faced with some obstacles. The need to overcome these obstacles will keep you focused on the external world and will give your action energy.

We want to answer these questions:

1   **Where am I?**
    Placing a monologue in a more public space can give you more choices and more imagined people to interact with. Placing a monologue in a more private space might give the person you are speaking to more freedom.

2   **Who am I talking to? What are they thinking/doing? What do I want them to think/do?**
    Always keep your feelings out of this; concentrate entirely on what your 'target' imagined person is feeling and on what you must make them feel in order to get what you want. Be imaginative about what your target is doing, because their action will always affect yours. If they walk away or ignore you, it gives you a strong reason to increase the energy of your actions. If they attempt to take your hand, burst into tears or pour you a drink, that might change both your action and your energy.

3   **What am I doing physically?**
    You will almost certainly cut some or even all of this rehearsal movement out of your audition performance, but in the early stages of the work, movement aids memory and keeps you from feeling physically trapped.

Below is my example for the Juliet monologue. This is my very first attempt and you will see it has a lot of detail. Although all of it is active, I've underlined the action that is <u>physical</u> action. Read this through carefully – it will take some concentration. Once we start rehearsing, we need to rehearse all the action separately from the text, just so that you can follow all the detail you might want to put into that second column. Some actors work best with this much detail, others prefer less, perhaps more decisive detail. You will have to judge for yourself what works best for you.

Text	Action	Who am I talking to?
Farewell! God **knows** when we shall **meet** again. I **have** a faint cold fear **thrills** through my veins, That almost **freezes** up the heat of life: I'll **call** them back again to **comfort** me: Nurse! What should she **do** here?	*I see the door close (my mother and nurse have just left)* *I see the window is open and I feel the cold night air* <u>*I go toward the door then stop.*</u>	Talking to Mother and Nurse
My dismal scene I needs must **act** alone. **Come**, vial. What if this mixture **do not work** at all?	*'Dismal scene' makes me <u>dig under my bed</u> for a bag (which holds the vial & a dagger)* <u>*I pull out the vial and look at it.*</u>	Talking to Romeo (imagining he is with me)
Shall I **be married** then to-morrow morning? No, no: this shall **forbid** it: **lie** thou there.	*The mixture looks like water. Suddenly I see my mother's face in water, looking happy because I'm married to Paris.* <u>*I get the dagger and lay it on the ground before me.*</u>	Talking to my mother (imagining she is with me)
Laying down her dagger	<u>*I pick up the vial again.*</u> *The water in it suddenly looks silver, like mercury*	

Text	Action	Who am I talking to?
What if it **be a poison**, which the friar Subtly hath **minister'd** to have me dead, Lest in this marriage he should **be dishonour'd**, Because he **married** me before to Romeo? I **fear** it is: and yet, methinks, it **should not**, For he hath still **been tried** a holy man.	*I see the friar coming toward me – I think he will do something harmful – I back away* *but instead he blesses me & I smile at him.*	Talking to the Friar (imagining he is with me)
How if, when I am **laid** into the tomb, I **wake** before the time that Romeo **Come** to **redeem** me? there's a fearful point! Shall I not, then, **be stifled** in the vault, To whose foul mouth no healthsome air **breathes** in, And there **die strangled** ere my Romeo comes?	*I rehearse lying down in the tomb. Then suddenly sit up. I imagine Romeo is with me. As I say 'stifled' my hand goes near my neck and I imagine having no air I realize that I am 'strangling' myself. I see Romeo smile & tell me 'you will live'*	
Or, if I **live**, is it not very like, The horrible conceit of death and night, Together with the terror of the place, –	*I show him how living could be worse. I try to remind him that love & night is good; death & night is bad.*	Talking to my image of Romeo, smiling at me.
As in a vault, an ancient receptacle, Where, for these many hundred years, the bones Of all my buried ancestors are **packed**: Where bloody Tybalt, yet but green in earth, Lies **festering** in his shroud; where, as they say, At some hours in the night spirits **resort**; – Alack, alack, is it not like that I,	*I point to a wall where all the tombs are. I point to the corner where Tybalt lies, and there is a bloody shroud. I move toward it but hear the bones whispering not to touch it. I pull the shroud away but there's nothing there. The spirits are 'resorting', and tormenting me.*	

Text	Action	Who am I talking to?
So early **waking**, what with loathsome smells, And shrieks like mandrakes' **torn** out of the earth, That living mortals, hearing them, **run** mad:– O, if I wake, shall I not be **distraught**, **Environed** with all these hideous fears? And madly **play** with my forefather's joints? And **pluck** the mangled Tybalt from his shroud? And, in this rage, with some great kinsman's bone, As with a club, **dash** out my desperate brains?	No one is taking me seriously – Alack! I practice lying down one more time and realize that the smells and shrieks would wake me – I sit up. Romeo doesn't hear, looks as if he would like to kiss me. I'm in no mood to be kissed – I want him to listen to me. Now I look down and see I am surrounded by bones. My forefather's bones (joints). I go to pull the shroud up one more time but something moves, so I pick up a bone. I look at it – I could kill myself with it.	
O, look! methinks I **see** my cousin's ghost **Seeking** out Romeo, that did **spit** his body Upon a rapier's point: **stay**, Tybalt, stay! Romeo, I **come**! this do I **drink** to thee.	This time I see that it is Tybalt. I step toward him. He knows Romeo is here, he looks for him. Then he turns to walk away. I want to protect Romeo so I call him back. When Tybalt turns he smiles – he thinks I am a coward. To spite Tybalt, I pick up the vial and drink.	Talking to Tybalt's ghost Talking to Romeo

Once you have completed all of your details, you need to practice it physically. Don't worry about words; in fact, don't worry about the text at all. If you've done your columns, fold them along the line so that in the early stages, you can only read the descriptions of what you are seeing and doing and who you are talking to.

With the description in front of you, rehearse the action of the whole thing as many times as you can, in the time you have left, and slowly try to get a feel for the order of all the action happening in this world. This isn't just to rehearse movement – you want to rehearse everything you see, as well as any physical movement you make. Be sure the imagined visuals are really strong. See what your 'target' is doing. Don't force any emotion and don't try to remember text. Just allow yourself to fully imagine what you are seeing and thinking and doing. I've learned from experience that in this work, you are probably going to have some emotional reactions to what you see or do – enjoy that and react easily and naturally to whatever comes up for you. Let whatever you imagine you see have an effect on you, but don't force anything. Keep your focus on the world around you.

Not all monologues will be as complex as the Juliet. Many are directed to just one person, and you will know exactly who you are talking to. Some are soliloquys (speeches spoken alone on stage) and they will require that you use your imagination to make sure that you have a very tangible imaginary target as you speak. If you are Iago, you may be talking directly to the audience – see them – but to give your monologue more range and pleasure, put people you know in the audience. Make them feel what you want them to feel. If you are doing Hamlet, talk to your father's ghost. Make him feel what you want him to feel.

SUMMARY

1   With a clean copy of the text, create your imagined world by answering these three questions:

  (a) Where am I?

  (b) Who am I talking to and what are they thinking/doing? What do I want them to think/do?, and

  (c) What am I doing physically?

2   Rehearse the action on its own until you feel the order of everything easily.

PHASE 3

REHEARSING AND PERFORMING THE MONOLOGUE

Of course, we've been rehearsing quite a lot in the process of preparation, but in a very indirect way. This indirect preparation is the perfect foundation for this next phase of focused rehearsal. Throughout the duration of this Phase 3, wherever you are in your timed practice, make a habit of using some time just before you go to sleep each night. Take 5 minutes before you turn out the light and 'read' through your monologue drawing. Don't try to force memory – throughout this phase you will start to feel like your mind wants to force you into trying to remember the monologue.

When working off book becomes irresistible (and it will), give in, but don't make yourself uncomfortable. If something doesn't come to mind easily, just reach for your drawing. When you are ready to let go of that drawing, you will. Often, when first getting off book, we find ourselves getting lost in the same spot. That usually happens between one unit or thought and another.

If you find this happens after you've let go of the drawing, it means that you need to strengthen your thought process at that point. There must be a reason why you move from one thought or action to the next, but you haven't quite figured that out yet. Rather than trying to force your memory over this 'blank spot', go back and think carefully about what happens in your imagined word that makes one thought or action move on to the next. There comes a point when using the drawing starts to get in your way, because you'll feel secure in the text. And when you do, remembering the text will feel automatic.

For the following sessions you'll find it helpful to use a timer and to keep a pen and paper nearby. Each session is followed by a relaxed, 'de-focused' time and you may want to make a note of anything that comes to you when you are in this relaxed mode.

At this point, you should have a working book that contains:

1 The two-column, 'bare bones' version of the text

2 The monologue broken down into units and accompanying pictures

3 Our full meter analysis

4 The two-column monologue showing patterns (in different colours)

5 A full drawing of the monologue

6 The three-column version of our imagined world, with physical action underlined.

We've had 24–29 hours of preparation time now, which means we only need about 6 hours of rehearsal with our working book. Ideally, we would spend 1–2 hours a day and not more. That means if we are working optimally, we should spend three to five days on this final part of our preparation.

The last work on meter

25 minutes: Physicalize the meter of the piece

1 HOUR

Don't go back to the text – use your drawing for this. It may take a few times to get through it all correctly, but time this and stick with it for 25 minutes. This is the last time we are going to pay attention to meter and all we want to do is get the rhythm of your piece into a nice, subconscious place. That will allow us to *stop thinking about it altogether,* which is where we want to be during performance.

Use the techniques described earlier: hit an imaginary punching bag on the stresses; walk around the room and stomp hard on the stresses, beat a pillow on the stresses – use a combination of these and just repeat for 25 minutes. If you get bored, make up a new way to physicalize.

5 minutes: Relax

When your timer goes off, take 5 minutes to just relax now. Don't distract yourself – close your eyes and relax. Don't try to think of anything. If thoughts or sounds come up, just let them. Don't force memory; just let thoughts 'happen'.

25 minutes: Vocal work and patterns

Turn to the 'patterns' page you've made. You are going to use this to create a vocal warm up exercise. Spend this time speaking out loud the repetitions, alliterations, oppositions, or any other verbal patterns you found in the monologue. As you read these patterns aloud, practice things you've worked on earlier: vary the effort levels with all of the consonants; try consciously sustaining vowel sounds in places that you haven't before or do all of the oppositions in level 10 consonant effort. You can practice the consonant/vowel exercises any way you like. You are not focusing on making sense here; you are focusing on making the most interesting sounds you can.

5 minutes: Relax

When your timer goes off, take 5 minutes to just relax now. Don't distract yourself – close your eyes and relax. Don't try to think of anything. If thoughts or sounds come up, just let them.

The last work on vocal colour

25 Minutes: Speech analyzer 'art'

1 HOUR

We are going to spend one last session with the speech analyzer and we are going to pay attention to what we SEE rather than what we hear. At this point you'll have a lot of instinctive ideas about the sound of the monologue, about what you want to do with it, about what you are seeing – but for this hour, we are just going try to enjoy SEEING how we sound, instead of hearing how we sound.

Open your analyzer and set your timer for 25 minutes. In order to get the most out of this exercise, try to let go of logic and just play with sound. Imitate people that you know. Speak like a pirate. Speak like an angel. Speak like the politician you hate the most. Imagine that your voice is a paintbrush. Use all the graphs on the analyzer and make as many different sound pictures as you can. Use diction effort and vowel sustains to create the widest range on the graph that you can. This isn't a logical exercise. This is just fun with sound. Be outrageous. We are about to head into rational, action-driven territory, so we want to have a last chance to play with sound before we start practicing those targeted decisions in rehearsal and performance.

5 minutes: Relax

When your timer goes off, relax for 5 minutes. Close your eyes. Think over the sounds you just made and think about whether any of them have stayed with you – the ones that made you laugh or were slightly embarrassing; the ones that sounded like someone you know; and the ones that you were surprised to find that you liked.

25 minutes: Putting action and bold sounds together

Choose some sentences from the monologue where the action is strong and clear. Think about these actions, and how you are using the words to affect the person you are speaking to, while you simultaneously increase the consonant effort level and allow yourself long sustains over some of the vowel sounds. Watch the speech analyzer, as you need visual feedback to see how your sound is adjusting once you start to make sense of the speech in terms of your active choices. Stay focused on trying to keep the widest range on the graph that you can while playing your actions with passion.

5 minutes: Relax

Once again, close your eyes and just clear your mind. If thoughts come up, let them. If there are sounds that you liked and they are still in your head, just enjoy the memory of them.

Putting text and action together

5 minutes: Vocal warm-up

Use some of the vocal warm ups you devised last session.

50 minutes: Put the action together with the text

Alternate doing the text of the monologue with physically practicing all the action. Let everything you see, and everything that happens have an effect on you. Add detail as you go along – if your written action says 'I see Romeo's face', make sure that you know exactly what you are seeing: exactly how he looks, what his expression tells you. Be very detailed. Some monologues don't have that much physical action, but keep going through what you are seeing/hearing/doing, and then alternate that practice with going through the text of the monologue. When you feel that you can comfortably do both together without losing any detail, do so. Some monologues have a lot of complicated action (my Juliet example certainly does!), and it may take a while to put action and word together in a way that retains all the detail, so don't rush the process. Your aim here is to get comfortable with doing both.

At this point it is very likely that feeling and imagination will start to make the monologue come alive – try to just let these things happen without forcing anything. This might be how you ordinarily feel when you are acting, or it might be different. But whatever happens, make sure you keep your focus outward, on your imagined world: on what you are seeing and on how you want to make whoever you are talking to feel. Remember – never talk to yourself. If you are doing a soliloquy, you may be talking directly to the audience – see them in a detailed way. Put people you know in the audience. Make them feel what you want them to feel. If you are Macbeth (doing 'She should have died hereafter' speech), maybe you can talk to Duncan's ghost – imagine that you want his sympathy and his forgiveness now that Lady Macbeth is dead. You can always imagine someone to talk to. Don't force *yourself* to feel anything – only concentrate on what you can make someone you are imagining/looking at feel. At least once or twice, go back to your 'action only' rehearsal, and keep thinking about how you can have an effect on this world/this person/the people that you are seeing.

5 minutes: Relax

When your timer goes off, again, take 5 minutes to just relax now. Don't distract yourself – close your eyes and relax. Don't try to think of anything. If ideas or sounds or parts of the text come up, just let them. Don't force memory, just let things 'happen'. This is where you allow your subconscious mind to enjoy the work. It is important that you don't try to steer things with your conscious mind. See what comes up to the surface and what remains with you.

Refine the action

60 minutes

1 HOUR

This is the point where you are going to start making some real decisions about what feels good; what feels right, instinctively. Try not to let your vocal or physical work get dull – because you are using a lot of brain power now to pull everything together, it is easy to sit like a lump or go back to some dull vocal habits. Resist that. Keep a pencil handy, because this is the point at which you are going to start refining the action/imagined world side of things. It is very likely that you will have added too much to the physical action column in your workbook. This is the point at which you want to reduce action if you can, and if it makes sense to do so. Physical action is helpful in the learning stage, but it can be distracting in performance. In an audition you want whatever action you use to feel organic and connected to the action you are playing, but don't allow it to distract from your power in playing those actions.

For the Juliet examples in Phase 2, I cut quite a lot of the physical action during rehearsal and left only:

- Pulling out a vial and looking at it
- Taking out a dagger and laying it down
- Backing away from the friar
- Raising my hand toward my neck
- Taking a step toward Tybalt's shroud
- Looking down at bones
- Stepping toward Tybalt's ghost

I kept in all the thought 'action' or thought processes about who and what I'm seeing, and how I want to affect what I'm seeing. But I cut out movements that seemed unimportant in relation to my acting objectives, or that I liked thinking about more than I liked doing:

Some monologues can be performed with little or no action and the amount of movement you keep remains up to you and your own artistic judgement. Too much movement will confuse people watching (and can sometimes look a bit amateurish). Too little might make you look stiff. Spend this hour trying things out – and remember that sometimes you may not want to cut an action entirely ('I take a swing at him' or 'I stroke her hair'), but just refine that action (I raise my arm as if I'm going to take a swing at him' or 'I move toward her').

The memory of your earlier physical action and the 'target' of your acting choices now should keep the world that you are performing in alive for you and should allow you to feel physically at ease in that world. It is helpful at this point to find someone who will watch you perform and give you some feedback on the movement that you've kept. But if you can't do that, just make sure that you are feeling a strong sense of belief in the world you've created and in the way you move in that world.

Find the pleasure

2 HOURS

After so much concentrated work on your monologue, it is time to find some pleasure. Oddly enough, pursuing pleasure in the work is the part of the rehearsal process that many actors never do. This may be because so often preparation is rushed and not done thoroughly, so finding pleasure in the work can be hard. If anything, the majority of the Shakespeare auditions I've watched have looked as if the whole experience was just hard work for the actor. The pain of trying to remember text or the difficulty of forcing an emotional reading, just seems to drain a performance of any relish or life. But we are in a position to find all the pleasure we can in the playing now. We've spent a number of hours getting right inside the structure and the world of the monologue. We know what we're talking about, we know what we are seeing and what we are doing, and that means the last step must be all about finding the joy in performance.

In a monologue like Juliet's, you might wonder how to find pleasure in playing a young woman scared to death and about to take something she fears might be poison. But as we know, these aren't the only things occupying her thoughts. So our final job is to look for pleasure in rehearsing and performing, wherever we can find it. Sometimes it lies in what we see or what we do. Sometimes it lies just in the beauty of the language and the way that it allows us to express ourselves with such range and precision or just the way it feels as we say it. Often it lies in knowing that we may never have the chance to defy, intimidate, seduce, inspire, frighten or dazzle someone in the real life the way that we can in Shakespeare's world. At other times, it is just having a sense of power here that we never have in our own, real world. And sometimes, it is just the sheer pleasure of speaking so well and being able to articulate our every feeling in such an amazing way.

Finding the pleasure should be easy, no matter what the circumstances of the monologue, because you are pretending to be in an extreme situation, but there are no real consequences from it. Therefore, the joy of being about to die or about to fight or about to fall in love or be betrayed comes from the very fact that you aren't really going to do any of those things. Instead, you are going to enter an imaginary world that feels as real to you as you can possibly make it and then you are going to play in these big, extreme circumstances with all the energy and focus that you have. This alone is a pleasure. Getting your way is a pleasure. Imposing your will on this imagined world is a pleasure. Making these people do what you want them to do is a pleasure. And being so prepared that you CAN do all this is a great pleasure.

Here are some of the things that I find pleasure in when I rehearse Juliet's monologue. I find they change from rehearsal to rehearsal, yet that doesn't matter. What matters is that I find pleasure in the big, scary world that I've created.

Farewell! God knows when we shall
meet again.
I have a faint cold fear thrills through
my veins,
That almost freezes up the heat of life:
I'll call them back again to comfort me:
Nurse! What should she do here?
My dismal scene I needs must act
alone.
Come, vial.

I love feeling strong and independent. I know I'm doing this to defy my mother.

What if this mixture do not work at all?
Shall I be married then to-morrow
morning?
No, no: this shall forbid it: lie thou
there.

I've never defied my mother before and this is going to teach her a lesson – don't meddle in my life!

Laying down her dagger

I enjoy outwitting the Friar. He tried to fool me and I love that I've found him out.

What if it be a poison, which the friar
Subtly hath minister'd to have me
dead,
Lest in this marriage he should be
dishonour'd,
Because he married me before to
Romeo?
I fear it is: and yet, methinks, it should
not,

I feel so safe when he blesses my forehead and I can see that he loves me.

For he hath still been tried a holy man.

How if, when I am laid into the tomb,
I wake before the time that Romeo
Come to redeem me? there's a fearful
point!
Shall I not, then, be stifled in the vault,
To whose foul mouth no healthsome
air breathes in,
And there die strangled ere my Romeo
comes?

Or, if I live, is it not very like,
The horrible conceit of death and
night,
Together with the terror of the place, –
As in a vault, an ancient receptacle,
Where, for these many hundred years,
the bones
Of all my buried ancestors are packed:
Where bloody Tybalt, yet but green in
earth,

Lies festering in his shroud; where, as
they say,
At some hours in the night spirits
resort; –
Alack, alack, is it not like that I,
So early waking, what with loathsome
smells,
And shrieks like mandrakes' torn out
of the earth,
That living mortals, hearing them, run
mad: –
O, if I wake, shall I not be distraught,
Environed with all these hideous fears?
And madly play with my forefather's
joints?
And pluck the mangled Tybalt from his
shroud?
And, in this rage, with some great
kinsman's bone,
As with a club, dash out my desperate
brains?

O, look! methinks I see my cousin's
ghost
Seeking out Romeo, that did spit his
body
Upon a rapier's point: stay, Tybalt, stay!
Romeo, I come! this do I drink to thee.

I love imagining Romeo's beautiful face
in front of me as I go through my fears.
I love his eyes and the way he smiles
at me.

There's a kind of perverse pleasure in
letting my fears run wild now. I'm alone
and I can say or imagine anything I
want. I know that Romeo will keep me
from all my terrors, but it feels good
to get it all out of my system. I take
pleasure in imagining the worst.

I love the way 'mandrakes', 'mortals'
and 'mad' sound when I say them.

I love the sense of really envisioning
all the terror. Someone might say I'm
being 'dramatic' but I don't care. It
is my life on the line and it is a great
release to say all my worst fears out
loud.

It makes me feel powerful to look at
Tybalt's ghost without being afraid.
I love defying him. I love the idea of
defying them all and running away with
Romeo.

As you see, finding the pleasure doesn't change what I'm seeing and it doesn't change what I'm doing when I aim my action at my various 'targets'. But it has made pursuing my actions and having an impact on the people and the things around me so much more pleasurable.

Spend your last 2 hours of rehearsal finding pleasure in the performance. Try not to do the full 2 hours all at once, but if you must, make sure you are taking breaks and allowing your subconscious mind to send up thoughts, images or sounds. Let it mull over the things you enjoyed.

What now?

We are at the end of our timed preparation and performance sections. If you are about to go and do your audition, you want to find one last thing: confidence. This is never easy, but if you genuinely have put 30–35 hours of work in, you can be pretty sure of one thing: the odds are that you now know this monologue better than anyone sitting on an audition panel. You know its quirks, you know its structure, and you know its rhythms. You know it inside out: you know its world and you know its pleasures. Let your advanced knowledge of this monologue keep you in a confident frame of mind. You've probably done more vocal and movement work on this monologue than on any other monologue you've ever done, and you feel comfortable with it. Imagine the audition going well. See yourself being offered the part/the place. Stay focused on positive things and when you feel your doubts creeping in, remember that you have deep knowledge of what you are doing and let that keep you confident.

Once you are no longer in a time-critical situation, go on to Phase 4, which will give you more practice and continue to increase your confidence when auditioning with a Shakespeare monologue.

I'M NOT IN A HURRY!

Deepening your practice

This is the section to turn to if you want to deepen your practice, spend more time on vocal colour, and get a bit more comfortable with the way Shakespeare structures a text. You will also find further examples of creating the imagined world of a monologue. This chapter is NOT TIMED, and is not part of your 35-hour audition preparation plan. If you are under time pressure, skip this section for now and come back later.

Laban efforts for voice

In our voice work in the first three phases, we looked closely at diction and sustain. Now, we are going to look at how Laban efforts can add to your ability to make bold vocal choices.

Most actors are familiar with Laban efforts as they relate to movement. Rudolf Laban was a movement practitioner who observed and analyzed movement very specifically in terms of weight, time and space. His analysis of these elements led to eight distinct efforts, which described the basic movement principles of all living beings. Of course, as his area was movement and dance, these eight efforts are generally applied to physical states. But many people now apply the study of Laban to voice – and I have found it extremely helpful when dealing with Shakespeare's language. Like so many things in life, Laban's system is relatively easy to explain but it can take years of practice to employ his ideas with sophistication and artistry. In workshops, however, I find that even an elementary understanding of Laban can help actors to add variation and colour quickly to their expressive sounds. So what we are exploring here is NOT a full consideration of Laban's wonderful movement techniques, but an adapted set of techniques that are based on his ideas, and applied to the voice.

We're going to start by considering the 8 basic efforts, but in order to do that, we have to understand that there are three basic categories common to all efforts, and these categories are weight, time and direction.

Weight

Weight can be thought of in terms of resistance to any force. When we talk about a 'heavy' weight quality in Laban effort, we are talking about a sense of very strong resistance to the force of gravity, or to an imagined force in any space. To understand this in physical terms you can try to imagine that you are attempting to move an imaginary wall. The heavier the wall, the more force and muscle you need. If you release your work of pushing the wall, of course, you are aware of how light your arms will suddenly feel.

In voice terms, we don't want to add any muscle tension to our vocal production. We can add muscle in the body, of course, to support sound, but what we really want to do is think a bit more metaphorically about transferring this description of movement to the voice – we know that when we talk about a heavy vocal quality, the sound is strong, and we may want to experiment with finding comfortable ways to make our voices sound strong or heavy. We also know that we can do the opposite: we can make our voices sound light.

EXERCISE 1

Work on these sentences, trying to make the 'weight' of the sound very distinct. Go through first and speak each sentence into your voice analyzer. In the first round, imagine the weight of your sound to be as heavy as you can (always monitor your effort and feeling and don't do anything that feels tight or constricted). 'Heavy' vocal sounds will almost certainly require the high level of diction we were working with earlier, along with a bit more vowel sustain. Now go through the sentences again and imagine the weight of your sound to be as light as you can make it. Don't let your 'light' sound mean that you come 'off 'of the voice (in other words, don't whisper). Also, make sure your 'light' sound still includes a crisp and clear consonant production. Finally, go through again and vary the light to heavy sounds. Use a speech analyzer and go through these sentences enough times that you can see what your 'heavy' vocal sound looks like and what your 'light' vocal sound looks like.

1 That you insult, exult and all at once, over the wretched?
2 Oh tiger's heart, wrapped in a woman's hide
3 Art thou king and wilt be forced?
4 Finds brotherhood in thee no sharper spur?
5 We are amazed and thus long have we stood
6 Where's that valiant crookback, Dicky your boy?
7 And my idolatrous fancy must sanctify his relics
8 And come you now to tell me that John hath made his peace with Rome?
9 The law hath not been dead, though it hath slept.
10 Plays such tricks before high heaven as makes the angels weep.

Time

Time can be thought of in terms of the sustaining exercise we did with vowels earlier. At the extreme ends of this category, Time can mean sounds either sustained or held for as long as we can reasonably, believably hold on to them (which feels like the duration of sound is a kind of continual flow), or it can mean sudden, staccato bursts of sound that don't flow and aren't connected.

EXERCISE 2

We've done an exercise in sustain, so here we are going to try one in which we make our sounds in the opposite way. This time, go through the following sentences and don't sustain any sound. Allow the words to just be short bursts of sound that aren't connected. Don't let your sound 'flow' in any way. Use a speech analyzer and go through these sentences enough times to feel that you comfortably understand what a sustained sound looks like and what a sudden, staccato sound looks like.

1 Edward's seven sons, whereof thyself art one.
2 Oh hateful hands, to tear such loving words!
3 Ah Gloucester, teach me to forget myself.
4 What, is't too short? I'll lengthen it with mine.
5 Now I do frown on thee with all my heart.
6 I left no ring with her – what means this lady?
7 I wonder how the king escaped our hands
8 Well, then, legitimate Edgar, I must have your land
9 Good madam, let me see your face
10 Out on thee! seeming! I will write against it!

Space

Space is very specific in Laban terms and relates to where and how we explore space all around us physically. We can look at this in speech terms by thinking about the pitch of our voices as having direction. We can speak in a flexible way (think of your sounds as being 'bendy' and flexible as you speak) or we can speak very directly – as if our voice only goes in one direction. A flexible voice explores pitch and rhythm and a direct voice speaks with minor variations of pitch. Perhaps the best example of the most direct voice would be older computerized voices, which had little variation in tone.

EXERCISE 3

A speech analyzer is great for this exercise, as you can clearly see the difference between a flexible and a direct sentence when spoken. Start by speaking the sentences below in a very direct way. Focus on keeping your sound repetitive- as if the sound is going in a straight line. Follow this with some exploration in flexible sound: explore all the range in your speaking voice, keep changing things up, as if your voice is 'bending' and turning; going in many different directions, and never staying on one true course. Do this exercise enough times to feel that you can see and feel the difference between your 'direct' voice (wave graph should be linear and not move much) and your 'flexible' voice (wave graph should be as wide as possible).

1 The honourable lady of the house – which is she?
2 So you must be the first to give this sentence, and he the first that suffers.
3 There is a vice, which most I do abhor and most desire should meet the blow of justice.
4 My lord, I did deny no prisoners.
5 Some heavy business hath my lord in hand, and I must know it else he loves me not.
6 In sooth I know not why I am so sad: it wearies me, you say it wearies you.

7   By my troth, Nerissa, my little body is aweary of this great world.

8   My lord I have remembrances of yours that I have longed long to redeliver.

9   But wherefore do you hold me here so long?

10   There is a tide in the affairs of men, which taken at the flood leads on to fortune.

Practicing using the Laban efforts for voice

Now that we have an understanding of the three categories, we can look at how they are mixed and combined to create Laban's eight efforts. The efforts are:

- Float
- Slash
- Glide
- Wring
- Dab
- Thrust
- Flick
- Press

This chart gives you a quick idea of what makes up each sound:

Effort	Time	Space	Weight	Think …
Float	Sustained	Flexible/wandering	Light	Kite flying slowly, uncertainly, think Sybil Trelawney in *Harry Potter*
Slash	Sudden/staccato	Flexible/wandering	Heavy	Zorro – zip, zip, zip in different directions
Glide	Sustained	Direct	Light	Think of ice skating/skiing
Wring	Sustained	Flexible/Wandering	Heavy	Wicked Witch in *The Wizard of Oz*: 'Wanna play ball scarecrow?'
Dab	Sudden/staccato	Direct	Light	Think of a painter dabbing paint on a canvas
Thrust	Sudden/Staccato	Direct	Heavy	Boom, boom, boom, like a series of quick punches
Flick	Sudden/Staccato	Flexible/wandering	Light	Glinda the good witch in *The Wizard of Oz*: 'Are you a good witch or a bad witch?'
Press	Sustained	Direct	Heavy	Think of Severus Snape in *Harry Potter*

EXERCISE 4

Keep the chart in front of you as you go through these practice sentences. At first, just exaggerate the sounds until you are sure you have the sound of each effort right and make sure you do the physical part of the exercise as well – that helps you remember the distinct sounds. Once you are sure of how the sound and the movements work together, go through the practice sentences just long enough to feel that you know the difference between each of the qualities pretty well in a practical sense. Do your best to make the sentences still sound like they make sense. What you are aiming to do here is to shake up completely the normal patterns of your spoken sound. Try to surrender to this exercise and just truly enjoy making sound.

Float Practice sentences (as you do these, 'float' around the room as if flying):

1   Oh were that all. I think not on my father.
2   Like bubbles on a late disturbed stream

Slash practice sentences (as you do these, slash an imaginary sword at different heights and in different directions):

1   Your grace shall pardon me, I will not back
2   They have the truth of this from Hero

Glide practice sentences (as you do these, pretend to 'skate' in one direction):

1   This battle fares like to the morning's war
2   When dying clouds contend with growing light

Wring practice sentences (as you do these, wring out a very heavy, imaginary wet blanket):

1   How happy some o'er other some can be!
2   O, yet for God's sake, go not to these wars!

Dab practice sentences (as you do these, dab tiny dots of paint on an imaginary canvas):

1   So many years ere I shall shear the fleece
2   So minutes, hours, days, months and years

Thrust practice sentences (as you do these, hit an imaginary punching bag):

1   It is the cause, it is the cause my soul
2   Let me not name it to you, you chaste stars!

Flick practice sentences (as you do these, flick imaginary flies off your arms, legs, and shoulders):

1   But I do think it is their husbands' faults
2   So are they all, all honourable men –

Press practice sentences (as you do these, imagine that you are pressing down hard as you iron a very wrinkled imaginary piece of linen)

1   In sooth I know not why I am so sad.
2   It wearies me, you say it wearies you.

Try some of these Laban qualities as you rehearse your monologue. Allow any sounds that you like to stay with you.

Unusual syntax

Words, the order of ...

Having spent time looking at meter and patterns in your monologue, you are probably feeling comfortable with the syntax of that particular speech. In this section we are going to look more generally at syntax and at some of the peculiarities of Shakespeare's writing, which should help to make you more comfortable the next time you approach a new speech or scene.

Shakespeare challenges our brain, and does so in good ways. Research has proven this.[1] When our brains encounter words or sentences that aren't immediately familiar, they go into a kind of 'higher gear' that puts us on alert and makes us more receptive to new and unusual things. Of course, this is a good thing, but when we are reading (and particularly when we are trying to make sense of things quickly), it doesn't FEEL good. It can feel extremely frustrating.

One of the things that we've come to see from our earlier work is that Shakespeare often changes what might feel like a logical order of words. 'Came there a Lord', instead of 'A Lord came there'. 'He will suspect us still', instead of 'He will still suspect us'. The way in which we structure language is known as syntax and often, more than Shakespeare's language, it is Shakespeare's syntax that confuses us.

---

[1] If you want to read some of the research I recommend: http://thereaderonline.co.uk/features/the-shakespeared-brain/ (accessed 24 March 2016)

The easiest way to understand what I mean by syntax is to think of Yoda in *Star Wars*. What distinguishes Yoda's way of talking is his unusual syntax:

Syntax has changed a lot in 400 years. So with Shakespeare, the word order is often turned around to our modern ear. This may have been because word order, or syntax, was mildly different in Shakespeare's day, or perhaps it is because Shakespeare wants to make the stress fall in a particular way in a line of verse. The reason isn't important to us here – but the effect is.

Our brains are amazingly adaptable, though, and are programmed to make sense of things when they can. This means that even a Yoda-type sentence like:

'love you I do'

makes sense to us, although of course:

'I do love you'

would strike us as the more usual order of the words in this sentence.

This is all pretty simple when the words are this familiar. However, it grows a little more complicated, when the words are either unknown or ambiguous. So we are just going to start our exploration around words we DO understand and see how much we can change their arrangement while retaining their meaning. Getting used to unusual syntax will make you more comfortable when you encounter it in Shakespeare.

Of course, Shakespeare uses simple sentences often. Some of these sentences use words that we are very familiar with and they are constructed in such a way that the word order feels pretty natural to us:

> *'Go in to him and fetch him out.'*
> *'Well, come to me tomorrow.'*
> *'Will you not tell me who told you so?'*
> *'I do but beg a little changeling boy'*
> *'What traitors have we here?'*

These are very simple sentences, but you could make them more complicated if you wanted to, just by moving the word order around. For example, the first one could be:

> **To him go in and fetch him out**

Or

> **Go in to him and out fetch him.**

I'm not suggesting that you would necessarily speak like this, but you *could* and people would understand you.

> **'As looks the mother on her lowly babe'**

Can be re-ordered as: **'As the mother looks on her lowly babe'**

> **'Environed he was with many foes'** (*Environed = surrounded*)

Can be re-ordered as: **'He was environed with many foes'**

> **'Yet so he ruled, and such a prince he was'**

Can be re-ordered as: **'Yet he so ruled, and he was such a prince'**

> **'And happy was it always for that son'**

Can be re-ordered as: **'And it was always happy for that son'**

Omitted things ...

Of course, it isn't just word order that makes syntax difficult –
sometimes Shakespeare 'implies' a word that isn't there. We saw this
in Ophelia's speech, where we had to insert a word in order to make
sense of a line:

> *Th'observed of all observers [is] quite, quite, down!*

This is something Shakespeare does with some regularity. Often, it is
done to get a line to fit comfortably into the rhythm of the verse. But
sometimes it seems to be a style choice. We do this ourselves quite a
lot in contemporary conversations, when we say: '[I'll] See you later!' or
'Answer a question [for] me.' But when the language isn't so familiar,
the missing words can sometimes be confusing:

> *If it be a suit from the count, I am sick, or not at home*
> *What you will, to dismiss it.*

Might feel a little clearer with the implied words added back in:

> *If it be a suit from the count, [say] I am sick, or not at home*
> *[Do] What you will, to dismiss it.*

The same is true of these lines:

> *Live a thousand years,*
> I shall not find myself so apt to die.

Could be:

> *[If I should] Live a thousand years,*
> I shall not find myself so apt to die.

And:

> *Stamp, rave and fret, that I may sing and dance*

Could be:

Stamp, rave and fret, [so] that I may sing and dance

These seem pretty simple, but some are harder and probably a bit debatable. I would say that:

Hard-hearted Clifford, take me from the world,
My soul to heaven, my blood upon your heads

Could be:

Hard-hearted Clifford, take me from the world,
[send] My soul to heaven, [and let] my blood [be] upon your heads

But others might not agree. That doesn't matter. What matters is that the line with added words makes more sense to me when I'm preparing a text for acting. And since I'm the one doing the monologue, what makes sense to me is what matters. It isn't, of course, that I *say* the added words. But the meaning of the implied words can be there when I'm speaking and the line, as written, stays beautifully within the iambic pentameter rhythm.

So when you are feeling confused about the meaning of a sentence, even when you know what all the words mean, try adding a word or two as I've done above, to see if it helps your understanding.

Some tricky pronunciations …

Missing words are only some of the things that we might have to search for when preparing our text. Just as often we find missing letters. Again, this isn't a completely historical practice – we do this every day when we say things like 'c'mere' or 'c'mon'. Sometimes in Shakespeare, the missing word is about keeping things in rhythm, and sometimes it is about a particular dialect, or it may signal a character's status. But we'll encounter it often enough to make things a bit confusing for us so it is wise to take a little time here to understand how we cope with missing letters when we are speaking the text. The only real rule is that you never change the sound of the vowel when a consonant is missing, so

you pronounce the line with the missing letter just as if the letter was
still there. For example:

Come on, i' God's name; once more toward our father's

sounds like:

Come on, in God's name; once more toward our father's

But you take the emphasis off the 'n'.

Similarly,

What one, i'faith?

sounds like:

What one, in faith?

But you take the emphasis off the 'n'.

When Goneril says:

We must do something, and i'th' heat.

It should sound very much like:

We must do something, and in the heat.

Although you would take the emphasis off the 'n', and the words 'in'
and 'the' would be spoken relatively quickly.

In *Henry V*, Hostess Quickly, describing the death of Falstaff, misses
out quite a lot of things – letters and words, which is very likely to be
Shakespeare's attempt to depict either a regional sound or her lower
status, and here she substitutes an 'a' where we would expect to see
an 'e':

*A' made a finer end and went away an it had been any christom
child; a' parted even just between twelve and one, even at the
turning o' the tide*

She's probably employing an early Cockney dialect sound, and much like the Cockney of today, she drops her 'h' and changes the long 'E' vowel sound from 'ee' to 'uh-ee', so the 'A's in this passage should sound like:

Uh-ee made a finer end and went away an[2] it had been any christom child;
Uh-ee parted even just between twelve and one, even at the turning o(f) the tide

When you first come across these things, they can seem quite foreign and confusing, but the more you read, the more you will grow used to the occasional missing letter or word. Some quick exercises should help to get you more comfortable with these ideas.

EXERCISE 1

Rearrange the order of these short sentences, which were mentioned above:

'Well, come to me tomorrow.'

_____

'Will you not tell me who told you so?'

_____

'I do but beg a little changeling boy'

_____

'A dire induction am I witness to'

_____

[2] 'an' has some unexpected uses in Shakespeare. If you ever see it like this (where it doesn't immediately make sense) try translating it to 'as if'.

'How smart a lash that speech doth give my conscience!'

_____

'What traitors have we here?'

_____

EXERCISE 2

Re-order these slightly longer lines and add in any implied words that make the meaning clearer for you:

'I am by birth a shepherd's daughter'

_____

'Assigned am I to be the English scourge'

_____

'Things sweet to taste prove in digestion sour'

_____

'The ripest fruit first falls, and so doth he'

_____

'Give me that glass and therein will I read'

_____

'And turn you all your hatred now on me?'

_____

'Have not to do with him; beware of him'

_____

'Needs must you lay your heart at his dispose'

_____

'Whilst I awhile obsequiously lament'

_____

Hath love in thy old blood no living fire?'

_____

Yet one more thing, good captain, do for me'

_____

'They love not poison that do poison need'

_____

'No word like pardon for kings' mouths so meet'

_____

'Something have you heard of Hamlet's transformation'

_____

'Of your philosophy you make no use'

_____

'There will I leave you too, for here comes one in haste'

_____

'I heard you were saucy at my gates and allowed your approach rather to wonder at you than to hear you'

_____

_____

EXERCISE 3

Insert the 'IMPLIED' WORDS and reorder if it helps to make sense of the line:

'Will you stay no longer? Nor will you not that I go with you?'

'I may do that I shall be sorry for'

'I will about it straight'

'Tomorrow in the battle think on me

And fall thy edgeless sword: despair and die'

'Feeling so the loss, I cannot choose but ever weep the friend'

'From enemies heaven keep your majesty'

'Assume a virtue if you have it not'

Woulds't have me weep? Why now thou hast thy will.

You'll find a lot of variations of these syntax issues in Shakespeare, and these quick exercises won't solve everything for you. But they should help you solve some issues, and the more familiar you are with them, the better prepared you are in reading a text for the first time.

POSSIBLE ANSWERS

Exercise 1
'Well, come to me tomorrow.'
> *Well, tomorrow come to me.*

'Will you not tell me who told you so?'
> *Will not you tell me who told you so?*

'I do but beg a little changeling boy'
> *I do beg but a little changling boy*

'A dire induction am I witness to'
> *I am witness to a dire induction*

'How smart a lash that speech doth give my conscience!'
> *How smart a lash doth that speech give my conscience!*

'What traitors have we here?'
> *What traitors here have we?*

Exercise 2
'I am by birth a shepherd's daughter'
> *By birth I am a shepherd's daughter*

'Assigned am I to be the English scourge'
> *I am assigned to be the English scourge*

'Things sweet to taste prove in digestion sour'
> *Things sweet to taste [can] prove sour in digestion*

'The ripest fruit first falls, and so doth he'
> *The ripest fruit falls first, and so doth he*

'Give me that glass and therein will I read'
  Give me that glass and I will read therein

'And turn you all your hatred now on me?'
  And now you turn all your hatred on me?

'Have not to do with him; beware of him'
  (Do) not have to do with him; beware of him

'Needs must you lay your heart at his dispose'
  You must needs lay your heart at his dispose

'Whilst I awhile obsequiously lament'
  Whilst I obsequiously lament awhile

Hath love in thy old blood no living fire?'
  Hath love no living fire in thy old blood?

Yet one more thing, good captain, do for me'
  Yet do one more thing for me, good captain

'They love not poison that do poison need'
  They that need poison do not love poison

'No word like pardon for kings' mouths so meet'
  For kings' mouths [there is] no word like pardon so meet

'Something have you heard of Hamlet's transformation'
  You have heard something of Hamlet's transformation

'Of your philosophy you make no use'
  You make no use of your philosophy

'There will I leave you too, for here comes one in haste'
  I will leave you there, too, for one comes here in haste

'I heard you were saucy at my gates and allowed your approach rather to wonder at you than to hear you'
  I heard you were saucy at my gates and [I] allowed your approach [in order] to wonder at you rather than to hear you

Exercise 3

'Will you stay no longer? Nor will you not that I go with you?'

> *Will you stay no longer? Nor will you not [allow] that I go with you?*

'I may do that I shall be sorry for'

> *I may do that for [which] I shall be sorry*

'I will about it straight'

> *I will [go] straight about it*

'Tomorrow in the battle think on me
And fall thy edgeless sword: despair and die'

> *Tomorrow think on me in the battle*
> *And [let] fall thy edgeless sword: [and there] despair and die*

'Feeling so the loss, I cannot choose but ever weep the friend'

> *[I] am so feeling the loss, I cannot choose but ever weep [for] the friend*

'From enemies heaven keep your majesty'

> *[May] heaven keep your majesty from enemies*

'Assume a virtue if you have it not'

> *[You must] assume a virtue if you have it not*

Woulds't have me weep? Why now thou hast thy will.

> *Woulds't [thou] have me weep? Why now thou hast they will.*

These exercises are only a start, but they give you an idea of how you can play with the order of Shakespeare's text sometimes to make meaning clearer when you are first trying to understand a piece. Of course, in performance, you must do the words as ordered but making the order a bit clearer for your own ear is helpful in the early stages of understanding a monologue.

Using verbs to analyze structure

We've been identifying description and repetition to get to the bare bones of a monologue. But there is another way to analyze structure, by isolating the verb phrases. I think any creative engagement with the text of your monologue is a good way to master it, and you may prefer this method. I test these ideas in practical settings all the time, and I've found that many actors prefer to use verbs to create their bare bones analysis. I think spending a little time on both will allow you to decide which is best for you. Instead of putting descriptive or repetitive text into parentheses, this method isolates all the subjects, verbs and objects. You will generally end up with a very clear idea of the bare bones, but will probably need to do some trimming if you want to avoid repetition.

This method is also helpful when you feel like you are looking at monologue that is just so full of description you don't know where to start. The opening of Titania's monologue in *Midsummer Night's Dream* is a good example of this:

> These are the forgeries of jealousy.
> And never, since the middle summer's spring,
> Met we on hill, in dale, forest or mead,
> By paved fountain or by rushy brook,
> Or in the beached margent of the sea,
> To dance our ringlets to the whistling wind,
> But with thy brawls thou hast disturb'd our sport.

The second sentence is very long and it is hard to navigate your way through when you first read it. But if you just look for verbs, you'll be able to get to the bare bones of the action quickly.

> These **ARE** the forgeries of jealousy.
> And never, since the middle summer's spring,
> **MET** we on hill, in dale, forest or mead,
> By paved fountain or by rushy brook,
> Or in the beached margent of the sea,
> **TO DANCE** our ringlets to the whistling wind,
> But with thy brawls thou hast **DISTURB'D** our sport.

Once we add a few words to clarify the meaning here, we have a very simple line of action:

> These **ARE** forgeries.
> And never **MET** we **TO DANCE**
> But thou hast **DISTURB'D** our sport

The verbs give us a quick pathway to the action here – and isolating verbs is one more tool that can help you see how a speech is structured, where all the action lies and who is doing what to whom. I think the reason so many actors prefer this method is because it follows the action so closely. If you have time in your preparation, you might want to try this method.

I'm going to do three examples first so that you get the idea, then I'm going to include two monologues to work with as an exercise.

When you start from verbs, you do NOTHING more than circle all the verbs you can find. If you are not sure about whether a word is a verb, just leave it – concentrate on the ones you are sure of.

Remember that there are ACTION verbs (run, shoot, play, cry, etc.), and there are STATE verbs (is, were, are, was, etc.). Often the STATE verbs are 'helpers' – they're helping to make the tense of the action clearer (He **was crying**, they **were running,** they **are playing**).

Some helpers also modify the verb in an important way – making them either positive or negative (I **can't help** you; you **must do** that, I **won't let** him, she **should not smoke**). You'll need to add these in so you can keep the sense of the speech.

In this exercise we are just going to find all the obvious action and state verbs first. Then we'll use 'helpers', subjects and objects. Sounds tough – but it ISN'T.

Example 1

Here's the opening of Portia's speech in the courtroom scene of **_The Merchant of Venice_**:

> The quality of mercy <u>is not</u> strain'd,
> It <u>droppeth as</u> the gentle rain from heaven

Upon the place beneath: it <u>is</u> twice <u>blest;</u>
It <u>blesseth</u> him that gives and him that takes:
'Tis mightiest in the mightiest: <u>it becomes</u>
The throned monarch better than his crown;
His sceptre <u>shows</u> the force of temporal power,
The attribute to awe and majesty,
Wherein <u>doth sit</u> the dread and fear of kings;
But mercy <u>is</u> above this sceptred sway;
It <u>is enthroned</u> in the hearts of kings,
It <u>is</u> an attribute to God himself;

So we begin with the verbs (and positive/negative modifiers) only:

_____

Is not

_____

Droppeth as

_____

Is blest

_____

Blesseth

_____

Becomes

_____

Shows

_____

Doth sit

_____

Is

_____

Is enthroned

_____

Is

_____

Now we are going to find objects, and we do this by asking the question 'what?' or 'where?' of each verb. So we'll start in this instance with 'is not what?' and carry on:

Verb	What?/Where?
Is not	strained
Droppeth as	rain
Is blest	twice
Blesseth	Him that gives/him that takes
Becomes	The monarch
Shows	(temporal) power
Doth sit	Wherein (therein)
Is	Above sceptered sway
Is enthroned	In hearts
Is	Attribute of God

You will probably note that the difficult one here is 'doth sit'. 'Doth sit what?' Isn't a very helpful question, but you can answer 'doth sit where?' and the answer is 'doth sit wherein' (but I've put 'therein' in parenthesis, because in this speech, wherein means 'inside of which', which is better translated here as 'therein').

Now I have my verbs in the right form and I've answered the question 'what' or 'where' for each, I need to fill in the subject (this is always whatever or whoever is carrying out the action). To find the subject, ask the question 'what?' or 'who?'. So, in the first line, above, we have 'is not strained' and the question then is 'WHAT is not strained?' The answer, of course, is 'mercy'. The next line is 'droppeth as rain', so we ask 'WHAT droppeth as rain?', and the answer, again, is 'mercy'. In this speech, Portia is describing mercy, so the subject is mostly mercy!

Subject	Verb	What?
Mercy	Is not	Strained
Mercy	Droppeth as	Rain
Mercy	Is blest	Twice
Mercy	Blesseth	Him that gives/him that takes
Mercy	Becomes	The monarch
(the King's scepter)	Shows	(temporal) power
Dread and fear	Doth sit	Wherein (therein)
Mercy	Is	Above sceptered sway
Mercy	Is Enthroned	In hearts (of kings)
Mercy	Is (an)	Attribute of God

Now I might want to tweak slightly (add a few words) for sense and now I have a very clear 'verb' version of the bare bones of the monologue:

Mercy is not strained.
It droppeth as the gentle rain
It is twice blest,
it blesseth him that gives and him that takes.
it becomes the monarch better than his crown;
His scepter shows temporal power
Wherein doth sit dread and fear
But mercy is enthroned in hearts of kings
It is an attribute of God.

Example 2

This is Phebe's speech from **As You Like It**. She is trying to get away from Silvius, who is in love with her. As you will see, she does not return his love!

I would not **be** thy executioner:
I **fly** thee, for I would not **injure** thee.

Thou **tell'st** me there **is** murder in mine eye:
'T**is** pretty, sure, and very probable,
That eyes, that **are** the frail'st and softest things,
Who **shut** their coward gates on atomies,
Should be **call'd** tyrants, butchers, murderers!
Now I **do frown** on thee with all my heart;
And if mine eyes **can wound**, now let them **kill** thee:
Now **counterfeit** to swoon; why now **fall** down;
Or if thou **canst not**, O, for shame, for shame,
Lie not, to **say** mine eyes **are** murderers!
Now **show** the wound mine eye hath **made** in thee:
Scratch thee but with a pin, and there **remains**
Some scar of it; **lean** but upon a rush,
The cicatrice and capable impressure
Thy palm some moment **keeps**; but now mine eyes,
Which I have **darted** at thee, **hurt** thee not,
Nor, I am sure, there **is** no force in eyes
That **can** do hurt.

Just to see them all out of the context of the monologue, here are all
the main verbs I found:

Verb		
Be	Frown	Made
Fly	Wound	Scratch
Injure	Kill	Remains
Tell'st	Counterfeit	Lean
Is	Fall	Keeps
Is	Lie	Darted
Are	Say	Hurt
Shut	Are	Is
Call'd	Show	Can

Now that I have this list, I'm going to back to each word and answer the question 'what' or 'where'? If the verb doesn't easily answer the question 'what?' or 'where?', then add some modifying words if you need to, so that it does. You might also have to modify some of these because they'll come out looking positive when they should look negative. I've bracketed the 'modifiers' in the list below. Make sure every verb answers the question 'what?' or 'where?' So, for the first word 'be', I have to add 'would not' so that the sense of the sentence is retained. And the answer to the question 'would not be what?' is 'thy executioner'.

Verb	What?/Where?
(Would not) be	Thy executioner
Fly	Thee
(Would not) injure	Thee
Tell'st	Me
Is	Murder in mine eye
Is	Very probable
Are	Soft
Shut	Gates
Call'd	Tyrants, murderers
Frown(on)	Thee
Wound	Thee
Kill	Thee
Counterfeit	To swoon
(Cans't not) fall	Down
Lie	Not
(to) Say	Eyes
Are	Murderers

Verb	What?/Where?
Show	Wound
Made (in)	Thee
Scratch	Thee
Remains	Scar
Lean (upon)	A rush
Keeps	Impressure
Darted	Eyes
Hurt	Thee not
Is	No force
Can	Do hurt

Now that we have our verb/object list, we are going to add a subject. Remember that the subject is whoever is doing the action. Sometimes longer sentences will include more verbs and objects than subjects – don't worry about that, only add subjects when you need to. Then modify things just enough to make sure that everything matches the sense of the monologue – and that mostly means making sure that positives are not negatives and the negatives are not positives. The modifiers are added in brackets below:

Subject	Verb	What?/Where?
I	(Would not) be	Thy executioner
I	Fly	Thee
I	(Would not) injure	thee
Thou	Tell'st	Me
	Is	Murder in mine eye
	Is	Very probable
Eyes	Are	Soft

Subject	Verb	What?/Where?
Eyes	Shut	Gates
Eyes	Call'd	Tyrants, murderers!
I	Frown (on)	Thee
I	Wound	Thee
I	Kill	Thee
Thou	Counterfeit	To swoon
Thou	(Cans't not) fall	Down
Thou	Lie	Not
	(to) Say	Eyes
	Are	Murderers
Thou	Show	Wound
I	Made (in)	thee
	Scratch	Thee
	Remains	Scar
	Lean (upon)	A rush
Palm	Keeps	Impressure
I	Darted	Eyes
I	Hurt	Thee not
	Is	No force
(in) eyes	Can	Do hurt

Now we have a very strange thing indeed, but if you read this out loud in its current SUBJECT–VERB–OBJECT state you will see that you actually have a version of the bare bones of the monologue. Of course, it is a bit repetitive – can you cut it further? *Would* you cut it further? But there are some words missing. What might you add to get a bare bones version you like?

I like the version below because it follows the action, cuts out the repetition and uses the fewest words possible, while still making sense of the speech. Thus, I would end up with something like this for my bare bones analysis:

I would not be thy executioner.
Thou tell'st me there is murder in mine eye.
Tis very probable that eyes, that are the softest things
Should be call'd murderers!
Now I frown on thee
And if mine eyes can wound, now let them kill thee.
Why now fall down;
Or if thou can'st not,
Lie not to say mine eyes are murderers!
I am sure there is no force in eyes
That can do hurt.

What is Phebe's main action?

She wants to prove to Silvius that she can't physically hurt him with her eyes, and she wants to be so rude to him that he'll leave her alone.

What is the balance of bare bones to 'parenthetical' language here?

It is about 50/50

What do you make of the parenthetical words and phrases here? Any strong imagery or metaphors? Do these tell you anything about Phebe or her world?

She speaks of frail, cowardly eyes (which might be what she sees when she looks at Silvius) she speaks of tyrants, butchers, murderers (which tells me that she lives in a pretty earthy domain) and she talks of leaning on a rush – rushes were used to cushion floors and beds in humble cottages, which suggests that Phebe lives pretty rustically.

Example 3

Let's do one more example before you try the two that follow on your own. This is Queen Margaret's speech in *3 Henry VI*, just before she orders the death of the rebel Duke of York.

> Brave warriors, Clifford and Northumberland,
> Come, make him stand upon this molehill here,
> That raught at mountains with outstretched arms,
> Yet parted but the shadow with his hand.
> What! was it you that would be England's king?
> Was't you that revell'd in our parliament,
> And made a preachment of your high descent?
> Where are your mess of sons to back you now?
> The wanton Edward, and the lusty George?
> And where's that valiant crook-back prodigy,
> Dicky your boy, that with his grumbling voice
> Was wont to cheer his dad in mutinies?
> Or, with the rest, where is your darling Rutland?
> Look, York: I stain'd this napkin with the blood
> That valiant Clifford, with his rapier's point,
> Made issue from the bosom of the boy;
> And if thine eyes can water for his death,
> I give thee this to dry thy cheeks withal.
> Alas poor York! but that I hate thee deadly,
> I should lament thy miserable state.
> I prithee, grieve, to make me merry, York.
> What, hath thy fiery heart so parch'd thine entrails
> That not a tear can fall for Rutland's death?

Now, I'm going to do the exact same exercise as before – I'll go through first and find all the action verbs. (Remember that you will have captured the verb correctly if you can answer the question 'what?' or 'where?')

Subject	Verb	What?/Where?
	Make	
	Stand (upon)	
	Raught (at)	
	Parted	
	Would be	
	Revell'd in	
	Made	
	(where) are	
	(to) back	
	(where) is	
	Look	
	Stain'd	
	Made issue	
	Water for	
	Give	
	Dry	
	Hate	
	Should lament	
	Grieve	
	Make	
	Parch'd	
	Fall for	

Now that we have verbs, all of which answer the question 'what', we can add the answer to that question in each case:

Subject	Verb	What?/Where?
	Make	Him
	Stand (upon)	Molehill
	Raught (at)	Mountains
	Parted	But shadows
	Would be	King
	Revell'd in	Parliament
	Made	Preachment
	(where) are	Sons
	(to) back	You
	(where) is	Dicky
	(where) is	Rutland
	Look	
	Stain'd	Napkin
	Made issue from	The boy
	Water for	His death
	Give	This (napkin)
	Dry	Thy cheeks
	Hate	Thee
	Should lament	Thy state
	Prithee	Grieve
	Make	Me merry
	Parch'd	Thine entrails
	Fall for	Rutland's death

Now I have my verbs in the right form and I've answered the question 'what' for each and I need to fill in the subject (this is always whoever is carrying out the action). Remember that there may be more than one action listed for a subject, so sometimes the field will be blank.

Subject	Verb	What?/Where?
Clifford and Northumberland	Make	Him
	Stand (upon)	Molehill
You	Raught (at)	Mountains
You	Parted	But shadows
You	Would be	King
You	Revell'd	In Parliament
You	Made	preachment
	(where) are	Sons
	(to) back	you
	(where) is	Dicky
	(where) is	Rutland
	Look	
I	Stain'd	Napkin (with blood)
Clifford	Made issue from	The boy
(if) Thine eyes	Water for	His death
I	Give	This (napkin)
(to) you	(to) Dry	Thy cheeks
(But that) I	Hate	Thee
I	Should lament	Thy state
I	Prithee	Grieve
	(to) Make	Me merry
(Hath thy) Fiery heart	(so) Parch'd	Thine entrails
Not a tear	Can fall for	Rutland's death

Now here, again, we have a very strange but very accurate beginning for our bare bones version. And, again, you can cut things that feel repetitive or add things that feel like they need to be added to make the best bare bones version you can. Have a try at this before you turn your hand to the exercises on the following two pages. From the work above I think I would end up with:

> Clifford and Northumberland,
> Make him stand upon this Molehill.
> What, was it you that would be England's king?
> Where are your sons to back you now?
> Look, York. I stained this napkin with the blood
> That Clifford made issue from the boy.
> If thine eyes can water for his death
> I give thee this to dry your cheeks.
> Poor York! But that I hate thee
> I should lament thy state.
> I prithee, grieve to make me merry.
> What, hath thy fiery heart so parch'd thine entrails
> That not a tear can fall for Rutland's death?

EXERCISE 1

We are going to practice doing a SUBJECT–VERB–WHAT?/WHERE? analysis. We'll start small, working our way up to more difficult monologues. I'm including a graph after each, just to make your life a little easier and I've followed that with a possible way to do the analysis. Do this in the order I did above – verbs first, 'what/where' second, subject third. I may have more boxes than there are verbs – don't worry about that! Just fill in the verbs you find. Remember that sometimes you can't fill in ALL the boxes!

This is York's response to Margaret, just before he is killed.

> That face of his the hungry cannibals
> Would not have touch'd, would not have stain'd with blood:

But you are more inhuman, more inexorable,
O, ten times more, than tigers of Hyrcania.
See, ruthless queen, a hapless father's tears:
This cloth thou dip'dst in blood of my sweet boy,
And I with tears do wash the blood away.
Keep thou the napkin, and go boast of this:
And if thou tell'st the heavy story right,
Upon my soul, the hearers will shed tears;
Yea even my foes will shed fast-falling tears,
And say 'Alas, it was a piteous deed!'
There, take the crown, and, with the crown, my curse;
And in thy need such comfort come to thee
As now I reap at thy too cruel hand!

Subject	Verb	What?/Where?

My verb analysis:

Subject	Verb	What?/Where?
Hungry cannibals	Would not have touched	That face
You	Are	Inhuman
Queen	See	Father's tears
Thou	Dip'dst	This cloth
I	Wash	Blood away
Thou	Keep	Napkin
	Boast	Of this
Thou	Tell'st	Story
Hearers	Will shed	Tears
Foes	Will shed	Tears
	Say	It was piteous deed
(thou)	Take	Crown, and, curse
To thee	Come	Such comfort
As I	Reap	

EXERCISE 2

This is Richard, speaking to his two brothers on the battlefield, just before the messenger comes on to tell them that their father, York, has been killed.

I cannot joy, until I be resolved
Where our right valiant father is become.
I saw him in the battle range about;
And watch'd him how he singled Clifford forth.
Methought he bore him in the thickest troop
As doth a lion in a herd of neat;
Or as a bear, encompass'd round with dogs,
Who having pinch'd a few and made them cry,
The rest stand all aloof, and bark at him.
So fared our father with his enemies;
So fled his enemies my warlike father:
Methinks, 'tis prize enough to be his son.
See how the morning opes her golden gates,
And takes her farewell of the glorious sun!

Subject	Verb	What/Where?

Here is my verb analysis:

Subject	Verb	What?/Where?
I	Cannot	Joy
(until) I	Be	Resolved
I	Saw	Him
	Range (in battle)	
I	Watch'd	him
he	Singled forth	Clifford
he	Bore	Him(self)
(as) Lion	In	herd
Bear	Encompass'd with	dogs
	Pinch'd	A few
	Made them	cry
The rest	Stand	aloof
(so)	Fared	Our father
(so)	Fled	His enemies
	Methinks	'tis prize
	To be	His son
(you)	See	how
Morning	Opes	Her gates
	Takes	farewell

Further example monologues

This last section gives you a few more examples of bare bones analyses and the 'imagined world' exercise. Often when I'm teaching a workshop on preparation, actors have told me that they find examples a good way to learn. I hope these further examples help to make things clearer for you and strengthen your confidence in doing your preparation.

I've tried to choose monologues that pose real challenges, and I've also looked for some that aren't used too often. The examples below are slightly under-used or perhaps not the best for audition (too short or too long). For these examples I'm going to use the 'parenthetical' method for creating the bare bones analysis.

Cressida, Troilus and Cressida, Act 3, Scene 2

This is a short monologue that is really challenging. When you look at the structure you can see why – throughout the piece she keeps changing her mind. Fortunately the language is pretty clear and you'll probably understand the piece pretty easily, even on first reading.

As you read the whole scene, you realize that her uncle, Pandarus, has come into the room before she delivers the speech – that's helpful when it comes to imagining exactly what's going on while she speaks.

This little speech has a lot of variations in text, depending on what edition you are using – I'm using the Arden here.

Bare bones

Hard to seem won: but I was won, my lord,
With the first glance (that ever)**–pardon me–**
If I confess much, you will play the tyrant.
I love you (now); **but till now, not so much**
But I might master it. In faith, I lie;
My thoughts were like (unbridled) **children, grown**
Too headstrong (for their mother.) **See, we fools!**
Why have I blabb'd? (who shall be true to us,
When we are so unsecret to ourselves?)
But, though I loved you well, I woo'd you not;
And yet, (good faith)**, I wish'd** (myself a man,
Or) **that we women had men's privilege**
Of speaking first. Sweet, bid me hold my tongue,
For (in this rapture) **I shall surely speak**
The thing I shall repent. See, (see)**, your silence,**
(Cunning in dumbness, from my weakness) **draws**
My very soul of counsel! stop my mouth.

Remember that the bare bones analysis is pretty subjective – you may disagree with what I have here, and that's fine. The structure of this speech is unusual because it follows very rapid changes of thought, and at first I thought there wasn't much to put in brackets. But the more I worked with it, the more I found. Once I finished, I thought about the three questions that always follow this analysis:

1 **What is Cressida's main action?**
   I think she has 2: she wants to maintain control. Even when she confesses her love, she immediately steps in to change her mind or modify what she's said. She also wants him to declare his love for her directly. When you read the scene you realize that they've been very careful with each other, exchanging metaphors and hinting at feelings. She wants a direct declaration, but she also wants control.

2 **What is the balance of bare bones to 'parenthetical' language here?**
   About 70/30 – I think this is because she's had enough of avoiding the truth of what they feel about each other – she wants direct and simple language at this point.

3 **What do you make of the parenthetical words and phrases here? Any strong imagery or metaphors? Do these tell you anything about Cressida or her world?**
   She only uses one strong metaphor – she compares her thought to unruly children. Apart from that she speaks of mothers, secrets, rapture, dumbness and weakness. It feels as if Cressida's world confines her somewhat – she's surrounded by what some see as women's weakness (perhaps what she also sees as women's weakness), but you sense that she would like to have more than just the man's privilege of speaking first. You can feel her dislike of weakness in this speech – even when she's changing her mind and begging him to kiss her.

At this point I have enough information to begin creating the imagined world of the monologue. Remember that this work is always going to be more interesting when you have knowledge of the play and particularly of what goes on before and after the scene. I've underlined the physical action here:

Text	Action	Speaking to?
Hard to seem won: but I was won, my lord, With the first glance that ever – pardon me – If I confess much, you will play the tyrant. I love you now; but not, till now, so much But I might master it: in faith, I lie; My thoughts were like unbridled children, grown	*I step toward him to reassure him, but he smiles, and I quickly realize that I'm giving too much away. I step back. I don't want to look at him here – I look away. I think I'm saying too much.* *On 'I lie' I'm going to defy him and I look straight at him. I'm surprised to see him looking so confused. As I talk about children he begins to smile, and for some reason that makes me think he's assuming too much, or taking me for granted.*	Troilus
Too headstrong for their mother. See, we fools! Why have I blabb'd? who shall be true to us, When we are so unsecret to ourselves?	*I blame my uncle for all this. He's a fool for putting me in this position. I step toward him, but he backs away. At least Pandarus looks down and seems to be ashamed of getting me into this mess with Troilus. I wait for an answer, but he gives me none.*	Pandarus
But, though I loved you well, I woo'd you not; And yet, good faith, I wish'd myself a man, Or that we women had men's privilege	*Troilus! I look back to him and now he's looking lost. Suddenly everything about him makes me want to touch him – his beautiful hair, his mouth, I let my eyes wander down to his shoulders and then I'm afraid I'll blush.*	Troilus
Of speaking first. Sweet, bid me hold my tongue,	*I look down, so he won't see and I ask him to stop me.*	
For in this rapture I shall surely speak	*Suddenly the room is uncomfortably quiet. He doesn't step toward me, so I step away. I look to my uncle quickly, who shakes his head as if he doesn't understand.*	
The thing I shall repent. See, see, your silence, Cunning in dumbness, from my weakness draws	*At 'see', I realize he isn't going to speak. I blame Troilus now, for refusing to stop me. Again I want to defy him, I want him to kiss me and*	
My very soul of counsel! Stop my mouth.	*I look straight at him, trying to command him at the end.*	

Hostess Quickly, Henry V, Act 2, Scene 3

This speech of Hostess Quickly is highly descriptive, as she's speaking of the death of Falstaff and her last few minutes with him. I'm guessing that the amount of description — and possibly her age – are the reasons I don't see this speech very often. But it holds some interesting challenges for our analyses. The first is the dialect that Shakespeare suggests here, and he elides a lot of words (not for meter purposes, because this monologue is in prose) and he drops the 'h' sound on the word 'he', which many modern dialects do.

There are some things we need to look up or think about – 'christom child' could mean either Christian or christened. In the third line, 'an' can be translated in your mind to 'as if'. There's much commentary about Falstaff babbling of 'green fields' and most of it concludes that what he was actually reciting was Psalm 23 about the Lord leading us into green pastures.

However, our greater challenge is simply the lack of action here, so we have to work quite hard to find some action that will keep us alive in this lengthy, descriptive memory. It helps to know that in this very short scene, she is with her husband, Pistol, Bardolf, Nym and the Boy.

Bare bones

Nay, (sure), **he's not in hell; he's in Arthur's bosom**, (if ever man went to Arthur's bosom). **'A made a finer end** (and went away) **an it had been any christom child; 'a parted even just between twelve and one** (even at the turning o' th' tide). **For after I saw him fumble with the sheets** (and play wi' th' flowers and smile upon his fingers' ends), **I knew there was but one way; for his nose was as sharp as a pen, and 'a babbled of green fields. 'How now, Sir John!' quoth I 'what, man! be o' good cheer.' So 'a cried out 'God,** (God, God!)**' three or four times. Now I,** (to comfort him,) **bid him 'a should not think of God;** (I hoped there was no need to trouble himself with any such thoughts yet). **So 'a bade me lay more clothes on his feet: I put my hand into the bed and felt them, and they were as**

**cold as any stone, Then I felt to his knees, and
they were as cold as any stone, and so up'ard and
up'ard, and all was as cold as any stone.**

1   ***What is Hostess Quickly's main action?***
    *I think the main action is to make everyone remember Falstaff
    as a good man, and not to be casual about his death. Certainly,
    she wants to defend his reputation. I have decided that she also
    wants to share in everyone's sorrow at his death, she wants to
    be tender with the Boy, and she wants feel her husband's love.*

2   ***What is the balance of bare bones to 'parenthetical'
    language here?***
    *About 70/30 – Although I think this is controversial and, as
    mentioned below, I could imagine that someone might see it
    closer to 90/10!*

3   ***What do you make of the parenthetical words and phrases
    here? Any strong imagery or metaphors? Do these tell you
    anything about Hostess Quickly or her world?***
    *There isn't much in parenthesis here, and there isn't much
    metaphorical language either. That tells me that Hostess Quickly
    doesn't inhabit a world where people talk in poetic ways. The
    only strong metaphor is her description of heaven as 'Arthur's
    bosom', and this is an interesting one. I had to spend some time
    researching this, and what Quickly really means is 'Abraham's
    bosom', but she confuses Abraham with the legendary king,
    Arthur. This reminded me that some of the glosses I read
    suggested that she misunderstood Falstaff, and when she
    thought he was babbling of green fields, he was actually reciting
    Psalm 23. When I put these ideas together I realize that although
    Mistress Quickly lives in a world where religion is powerful, she
    herself is probably not terribly religious in any conventional way.
    It is unlikely she can read, but she knows the legend of Arthur.
    And it seems to me that in her mind, paradise is NOT with
    Abraham, but with the legendary king.*

I've found this a tough 'bare bone' analyses, simply because I can
imagine an argument that says EVERYTHING in this monologue is

necessary; there is little repetition and description is the whole point of the monologue. Still, I offer this view as my own and even if, in the end, I hadn't found anything to put in brackets, the exercise of trying to do that would have immensely helped my understanding of the piece and its structure.

Similarly, I've found the action side tough, because on one level the whole short passage is just a sad memory. But we know that when we are doing an audition monologue, we need to keep things as active as possible, and we need to give ourselves a lot of detail to focus on. That means being pretty creative when it comes to filling in the action side of things!

Text	Action	Speaking to?
Nay, sure, he's not in hell; he's in Arthur's bosom, if ever man went to Arthur's bosom. 'A made 'a finer end and went away an it had been any christom child; 'a parted even just between twelve and one, even at the turning o' th' tide. For after I saw him fumble with the sheets and play wi' th' flowers and smile upon his fingers' ends, I knew there was but one way; for his nose was as sharp as a pen, and 'a babbled of green fields. 'How now, Sir John!' quoth I 'what, man! be o' good cheer.' So 'a cried out 'God, God, God!' three or four times. Now I, to comfort him, bid him 'a should not think of God; I hoped there was no need to trouble himself with any such thoughts yet. So 'a bade me lay more clothes on his feet: I put my hand into the bed and felt them, and they were as cold as any stone; then I felt to his knees, and they were as cold as any stone, and so up'ard and up'ard, and all was as cold as any stone.	*I'm going to punish Bardolf for suggesting that Falstaff might be in hell, so I flick my tea towel at him and maybe at Nym, as I remind all of them that Falstaff was a good, Christian man. Now they look ashamed. Good.* *I've just remembered that Pistol once said Falstaff would only ever die in the morning, when he had a hangover. I put my hand on Pistol's arm as I explain when he died.* *I've just realized that the Boy is with us and he may not have seen death yet. I make a move to ruffle his hair, but he backs away, so I gently explain the signs of impending death to him. Now everyone looks miserable. So I try to lift their spirits a bit – I know they will see the joke in my telling Falstaff not to 'trouble himself' with God.* *As I tell the saddest part – feeling his cold flesh – I can see Falstaff's huge smile and his warmth, and suddenly I long to have my warm husband hold me in his arms, so I move toward him.*	Bardolf Pistol The Boy Pistol, Bardolf, Boy Pistol

It is likely that in my final rehearsals I will refine what little action there is here (flicking tea towel, reaching for the Boy, moving toward Pistol) into very little, or perhaps even no physical action, apart from moving my gaze around all of them. But for early rehearsal purposes it is very helpful to keep it all in. Remember that when you are doing an 'action' rehearsal, it isn't only physical – you must go through all the thought process as well.

3 Henry VI, Act 3, Scene 1

Some monologues make it hard to imagine who you are speaking to or what you are doing. As advised earlier, you might want to rethink your choice. But if you have absolutely decided that you must do the monologue, then you have your work cut out for you. The fact that it isn't immediately clear who you are talking to, doesn't mean you shouldn't have someone to speak to. The fact that you can't think of any physical action doesn't mean that you don't imagine any physical action – it just means you have to be more creative, and you have to work much harder at it. But if you choose to do a monologue where the action or the 'target' isn't immediately obvious, that work will certainly pay off in performance.

This is King Henry VI apparently talking to himself when he thinks he is alone. But if we think about our own real life experience of doing a very lengthy monologue when we are on our own, we know that we tend to do them when we are 'rehearsing' an argument we are about to have, or replaying one we've just had, and this time we are remembering all the things we meant to say, but didn't. At these moments, we tend to 'talk to ourselves' with real passion – because we are imaging that someone else is there! This is why it is important for actors, always, to have a 'target' – someone they are talking to, and something they are trying to make that person feel.

For this monologue, I'm going to draw on my knowledge of the *Henry VI* trilogy, and I've decided that there's only one person Henry ever wholly trusts: his Lord Protector, the Duke of Gloucester. As young Henry's 'protector', the Duke sought to help Henry become a strong King. Henry now finds himself usurped and abandoned, alone in a forest, hiding from the world. So I will imagine that Henry knows just how badly things have gone in Gloucester's absence, but he is trying to convince the Duke that all may yet be well. By the end, of course, he realizes that it won't, so overall I think he is trying to imagine how the

Duke would advise him in this situation. He also speaks of Margaret, Warwick and the French king, Lewis, as if they are right in front of him, so at times he is speaking to them too, and must imagine how they will hear his words.

> **My queen and son are gone to France for aid;**
> **And,** (as I hear, the great commanding) **Warwick**
> **Is thither gone, to crave the French king's sister**
> (To wife) **for Edward: if this news be true,**
> **Poor queen** (and son,) **your labour is** (but) **lost;**
> **For Warwick is a subtle orator,**
> **And Lewis** (a prince) **soon won with moving words.**
> **By this account then Margaret may win him;**
> **For she's a woman to be pitied much:**
> (Her sighs will make a battery in his breast;
> Her tears will pierce into a marble heart;
> The tiger will be mild whiles she doth mourn;
> And Nero will be tainted with remorse,
> To hear and see her plaints, her brinish tears).
> **Ay, but she's come to beg, Warwick to give;**
> **She,** (on his left side,) **craving aid for Henry,**
> **He,** (on his right,) **asking a wife for Edward.**
> **She weeps, and says her Henry is deposed;**
> **He smiles, and says his Edward is install'd;**
> **That she,** (poor wretch,) **for grief can speak no more;**
> **Whiles Warwick** (tells his title, smooths the wrong,)
> **Inferreth arguments of mighty strength,**
> **And** (in conclusion) **wins the king from her,**
> (With promise of his sister, and what else,
> To strengthen and support King Edward's place.)
> **O Margaret, thus 'twill be; and thou, poor soul,**
> **Art then forsaken**(, as thou went'st forlorn)!

1   *What is Henry's main action?*
     I think the main action is initially to convince his (now dead) Uncle Gloucester that things may still turn out well if France comes to their aid, and to imagine how he would have explained all to Gloucester. I think he hopes that if he explains it well, his imaginary Gloucester can give him some advice.

That makes this monologue quite interesting, because by the time he gets to final third of the monologue, once he's clearly imagined the scene, he realizes that poor Margaret doesn't have a chance. So while his opening action is to convince in a positive way, his closing action is to forget about Gloucester and to comfort the lost Margaret that he sees in his mind.

2 **What is the balance of bare bones to 'parenthetical' language here?**
About 70/30 in favour of active language.

3 **What do you make of the parenthetical words and phrases here? Any strong imagery or metaphors? Do these tell you anything about Henry or his world?**
His main metaphor is in describing the power of sighs and tears – he sees sighs having the power to 'batter'; tears, he thinks, can 'pierce'. His other main metaphor is to see King Lewis as a tiger (although he also calls him Nero). This tells me something of the faith he has in the persuasive power of tears and sighs (although even he finally realizes that they will be useless), and something of the way he sees animal fierceness in other kings. In the end Henry realizes too late that the 'divine right' of his claim to the throne he has lost will never be as useful to a powerful foreign monarch as immediate advantages of alliance with a seated King. His world seems to be about absolute power and absolute loss of that power.

The monologue is very clear, and that means you won't have to work hard to make sense of it – either for yourself or for your listener. But you WILL have to work hard to make it interesting: to physicalize it and to find someone to talk to. Because this is a history play, I found it helpful to read a little of the history of the real Henry VI, who it turns out may have suffered from depression and/or schizophrenia. That notion unlocked a little of the mystery of this speech – there's something about the way that Henry's imagination seems to switch quickly from seeing one person and then another, and the way that his hopeful beginning is so quickly undone, that makes me wonder if he isn't, at this very extreme point in his life, having a little mental disturbance. I believe now that he might truly think he is seeing his dead uncle, his enemy Warwick, King Lewis, and his poor wife. That imaginary idea helps to give this speech life.

Text	Action	Speaking to?
My queen and son are gone to France for aid; And, as I hear, the great commanding Warwick Is thither gone, to crave the French king's sister To wife for Edward: if this news be true, Poor queen and son, your labour is but lost;	I'm holding my prayer book, praying. I look up and see my Uncle – he's disappointed at the mess I'm in. I can see his sadness. I step toward him. In front of me I imagine Warwick, looking triumphant. I put my prayer book away. I look straight at him and accuse him of being 'subtle' – sly.	Duke of Gloucs. Warwick
For Warwick is a subtle orator, And Lewis a prince soon won with moving words. By this account then Margaret may win him; For she's a woman to be pitied much: Her sighs will make a battery in his breast; Her tears will pierce into a marble heart;	At the mention of Lewis I remember that I have a letter from him that I have kept for years, I look in my pockets for it – it is gone. I don't worry about that – I remember that the letter said he would always be there to help, I believe now that I can convince the Duke she will be okay.	Duke of Gloucs.
The tiger will be mild whiles she doth mourn; And Nero will be tainted with remorse, To hear and see her plaints, her brinish tears.	I can see Margaret now, I want to give her the letter but I don't have it, so I find my rosary instead. I want to 'cheer' her on, so I step toward her.	
Ay, but she's come to beg, Warwick to give; She, on his left side, craving aid for Henry, He, on his right, asking a wife for Edward. She weeps, and says her Henry is deposed; He smiles, and says his Edward is install'd; That she, poor wretch, for grief can speak no more;	I see Warwick step forward, now I stop and see them in front of me – Lewis in the middle, Margaret on his left, Warwick on the right. I move toward Margaret, holding out my rosary. I need God's help. I want to shame Warwick, I want him to see that God is on my side – on Margaret's side.	
Whiles Warwick tells his title, smooths the wrong, Inferreth arguments of mighty strength, And in conclusion wins the king from her,	I use the words 'smooth' 'inferreth' to shame Warwick further, but I see him turn away from me.	
With promise of his sister, and what else, To strengthen and support King Edward's place.	I watch Lewis shake Warwick's hand and I drop my rosary. It slips through my hand.	
O Margaret, thus 'twill be; and thou, poor soul, Art then forsaken, as thou went'st forlorn!	I step toward Margaret, she is in a heap on the floor. I put my hand on her head.	Margaret

It has been difficult to find much physical activity, but the activity I've imagined feels helpful for me in terms of tying action to the text. It is simple – the dropping of a rosary, looking for a lost letter – but these are things that suggest a lot to me and they will also help me keep the overall structure of the speech in my head.

I've chosen some very hard monologues for these examples, partly to demonstrate that even the toughest monologues or soliloquys can have vibrant action happening around them. If you have the freedom to choose your own monologue for an audition, you will make your experience easier if you choose a speech for which you feel like you can easily imagine the external world. If you are an actor who likes a lot of challenge and autonomy, though, these tougher pieces can be an enjoyable creative puzzle.

Some final questions

If you bought this book while under time pressure, you probably jumped straight into the preparation and may only be reading this brief, concluding section at the point where you've had time to think about the process described in this book. And I can imagine that you may have the kind of questions that come up so often when I teach this in practical workshop settings. In anticipation of those questions, I thought I might include them and address them here.

What about acting?

This is a reasonable question, since I never actually address acting in this book. I talk about imagination, and I talk about having an impact on the imagined world around you, and on how you mean to make things happen in that world. I ask you to make things happen by changing the people you are (in your imagination) talking to. I talk about finding pleasure in the work and about trying to use both conscious and unconscious modes of thinking. I also insist that you never include your own feelings when you are imaging the world around you, since I know that your feelings will come along naturally when you are actively engaged in changing the ideas/opinions/world around you. For me, these things combined, are what actors are doing when they are acting.

What about character?

Another reasonable question, as I never address character in this book either. I talk about how, when you are engaged in all the activities of rehearsing and performing your monologue, you interact with a fully imagined world. Every choice you make in those interactions are what, finally, determine character. Particularly in an audition situation I think that the idea of 'character' can be an unnecessary worry for an actor. Auditions aren't the place to do anything extreme – this is why actors are advised to do a speech that suits THEM. Auditors generally are trying to figure out who you are and how you work. Showing up in a cape, a fake nose and hunchback will certainly tell them something about you, but probably not what you want them to know. Character will emerge organically out of the choices you make and out of the way in which you interact with the world. Those choices and that inter-action will always be based on your understanding of who Lady Anne, Macbeth or Rosalind might be.

Why so much detail in preparation?

An audition is very different from the experience of acting in a play. When we are working with a company, a director, a set, costume, lighting, we have a vibrant and inspiring world to react within. Other actors in the company surprise, delight, frustrate us – and we respond accordingly. We have weeks to explore the world of the play and the full journey of the role we are cast in.

In an audition, we need to create all of this for ourselves. We need to play the monologue the way we would if we had a company, a director and weeks of rehearsal and creative collaboration. And that requires a very detailed preparation. But doing this great detail has one superb advantage for the auditioning actor: the more imagined detail we can see and respond to, the more working memory/cognitive energy we are expending in the *right* way. The less we have to see and respond to, the more free space in our working memory/cognitive engine house and we'll undoubtedly use that space in the *wrong* way. If we have free cognitive space, we'll use it to:

- Critique ourselves as we go along

- Notice what the panel are doing
- Become distracted and lose focus
- Become self-conscious
- Allow our nerves to swamp our brains and go 'blank'

Creating and rehearsing imagined detail allows you to crowd all of that out of your working memory space, and keeps you focused. Well-imagined detail is the greatest help to an auditioning actor.

Why do you advise against using sites like 'No Fear Shakespeare'?

For a young reader, trying to get through Shakespeare for the first time in an English class, sites like this may be helpful. But if an actor uses a 'contemporary translation' of the texts, he or she might just as well hire another actor to do their audition for them. A significant part of your audition performance is the unique way in which you interpret the text. Shakespeare's writing is so beautifully ambiguous, he leaves much room for your unique vision. Having some unknown writer 'translate' his language for you isn't just lazy – it collapses all of your possibilities and sometimes forces an interpretation on you. You can see that in this brief exchange between Ophelia and Hamlet:

Ophelia
What means your lordship?
Hamlet
That if you be honest and fair,
Your honesty should admit no

Discourse to your beauty.

Ophelia
My lord, what are you talking about?
Hamlet
I'm just saying that if you are good and beautiful, your goodness should have nothing to
Do with your beauty[3]

You can see that the editor/writer hasn't just 'translated' this language into contemporary idiom. They have decided that Hamlet is hedging himself by starting his second line with the words 'I'm just saying

---

[3] Available online: http://nfs.sparknotes.com/hamlet/page_142.html

that …' It would be difficult for the actor playing Hamlet to add this modifying phrase without thinking that perhaps he had gone too far in what he said to Ophelia earlier. In contemporary idiom, the phrase 'I'm just saying that …' is something we use when we see that we've upset someone with our bluntness and we want to rephrase and (maybe) calm them down. But Shakespeare doesn't give Hamlet any 'hedging' phrase here – he carries straight on with his very direct point – that Ophelia's beauty will probably corrupt her honesty.

No Fear Shakespeare is not aimed at actors, and actors use it at their peril.

SUMMARY

Auditioning is a significant part of the actor's life. You will spend much of your time in preparation for auditions, and you will learn as you gain experience. Some of that experience needs to be gained 'under fire' – that is to say, you need the full experience of going through auditions to get better at coping with the neuro-physical effects of the fear they induce. But you also need to gain experience by keeping your skills topped up and by widening your knowledge. Most actors have at least two classical monologues in the portfolio, and that should be your aim. Having worked your way through the process in this book once, you now have the skills to prepare a second and a third monologue in far less time, because you'll be working through the parts in Phases 2 and 3, only. Each time through you'll find yourself feeling more comfortable with the language, more confident in finding the pleasure in doing them and far less frightened when asked to prepare a Shakespeare monologue. I hope this process will make the experience of preparation much more enjoyable for you and that it helps you discover all the wonderful possibilities alive in his work.

APPENDIX

The *Harry Potter* MONOLOGUE LISTS

I've come to realize, in discussing this idea with many people that this could make a great parlour game. It is almost inevitable that people will end up disagreeing with where I've put some characters, since the way that we read a character's personality can be a pretty subjective thing. Still, the point of this list is not to create an exact match between J. K. Rowling's characters and Shakespeare's, but simply to match some character attributes or types. I hope this will help actors narrow down the field when they're looking for monologues that might suit them.

Depending on how you answered the Harry Potter *casting questions on pp. 88–92, these monologues should be a good starting point for your explorations.*

In the lists below, I've decided to stick with twenty lines as a minimum monologue. There are a few women's monologues that are shorter than this, and since women's monologues are far less frequently found, I've added those to the lists. But the men's monologues are all at least twenty lines long. This means, of course, that there are many other good monologues of eighteen or nineteen lines, but in the interests of economy of space I've had to stick with twenty.

Some of the monologues are regularly used, even though they require a bit of cutting and pasting from you. I've indicated where these are. Some characters have more than one monologue in a given scene – make sure you read the whole scene to see if there is more than one monologue. And some characters suit more than one character type and therefore show up in more than one place – for example, Helena from All's Well That Ends Well *shows up in the lists for young and old Hermoine as well as the list for Nymphadora Tonks.*

Women

Professor McGonagall – *strong character: wise, reliable, at times quite harsh, but always good-hearted and loving (even when she hides it). She's not a character you want to cross, and she doesn't suffer fools at all. Mature. Good for actors comfortable playing characters who are: Decisive, confident and empowered and who tend to intellectualize emotion. Driven by intellectual curiosity and the need to defend the innocent.*

> **Abbess** (Aemelia) (5.1) **Comedy of Errors**
> **Volumnia** (1.3; 3.2 – cut Menenius' line; 5.3) **Coriolanus**
> **Duchess of Gloucester** (2.2) **Richard II**
> **Paulina** (3.2) **The Winter's Tale**

Mrs Weasley – *kind and maternal, but also wise and willing to face up to scary challenges. She's like a mother lion if anyone she loves is threatened and she has a lot of strength to draw upon when a situation gets tough. Young Adult or Mature. Good for actors comfortable playing characters who are: vulnerable, trusting, social, who tend to display emotion freely, and are driven by love and care of others.*

> **The Countess** (1.3; 3.4 – cut Steward's second line) **All's Well That Ends Well**
> **Mariana** *(3.5)* **All's Well That Ends Well**
> **Mistress Quickly** (2.1) **Henry IV, Part 2**
> **Hostess Quickly** (2.3) **Henry V**
> **Calpurnia** (2.2 – cut Caesar's lines) **Julius Caesar**
> **Emilia** (4.3) **Othello**
> **Nurse** (1.3) **Romeo and Juliet**
> **Hermoine** (3.2) **The Winter's Tale**
> **Two Queen** (1.1) **Two Noble Kinsmen**

Young Hermoine Granger – *strong all round leading action heroine: wise, compassionate and brave. She has a powerful sense of right and wrong and is instinctively drawn toward goodness. Juvenile or Young Adult. Good for actors comfortable playing characters who are:*

decisive, open-ended and careful, who display emotion reservedly or freely and are driven by passion, curiosity and desire for justice.

Helena (1.1; 1.3; 3.2) *All's Well That Ends Well*
Rosalind (3.2; 3.5; 5.2) *As You Like it*
Imogen (3.2; 3.4 – along with 'Why I must die', many of the passages can be edited into longer monologue length; 3.6; 4.2) *Cymbeline*
Helena (1.1; 2.2; 3.2) *Midsummer Night's Dream*
Marina (4.6 – cut Boult's line) *Pericles, Prince of Tyre*
Juliet (2.2; 2.5; 3.2; 4.3) *Romeo and Juliet*
Katharina (4.3; 5.2) *Taming of the Shrew*
Viola (2.2) *Twelfth Night*
Julia (1.2; 2.7 – cut Lucetta's line; 4.4) *Two Gentlemen of Verona*

Older Hermoine Granger – *strong all round leading action heroine: wise, compassionate, brave. She has all the characteristics of her younger self, but grows more complex and cautious as she matures. Still intellectual, but increasingly more in touch with her emotion and her more loving self as she matures. Juvenile or Young Adult. Good for actors comfortable playing characters who are: decisive, vulnerable, careful, with tendency to display emotion freely or even extravagantly at times. Driven by curiosity, desire for love and justice.*

Helena (1.1; 1.3; 3.2) *All's Well That Ends Well*
Luciana (3.2) *Comedy of Errors*
Lady Percy (2.3) *Henry IV, Part 1*
Lady Percy (2.2) *Henry IV, Part 2*
Portia (2.3) *Julius Caesar*
Princess (2.1; 4.1; 5.2) *Love's Labour's Lost*
Portia (1.2; 3.2; 3.4; 4.1) *Merchant of Venice*
Isabella (2.2 – cut Lucio & Provost lines; 2.4; 2.6; 5.1 – 'Most strange....' – cut Duke Vincentio's lines) *Measure for Measure*
Beatrice (4.1 – 'Is he not approved …' to 'woman with grieving' – cut Benedick's lines) *Much Ado About Nothing*
Hero (3.1 – 'Good Margaret, run ...' to 'hear our conference' – cut Margaret's line) *Much Ado About Nothing*
Juliet (2.2; 2.5; 3.2; 4.3) *Romeo and Juliet*

Silvia (4.3) *Two Gentlemen of Verona*

Ginny Weasley – *the girl-next-door: dependable, attractive, smart and definitely 'marriage material'. Stronger than she looks, but allows others to take the lead. Juvenile or Young Adult. Good for actors comfortable playing characters who are: vulnerable, trusting, self-sacrificing, with a tendency to be reserved about displaying emotion in social circumstances. Driven by love and desire.*

> **Adriana** (2.1 – cut Luciana's line; 2.2; 5.1) *Comedy of Errors*
> **Ophelia** (2.1 – cut Polonius' lines; 3.1) *Hamlet*
> **Hero** (3.1 – 'Good Margaret, run...' to 'hear our conference' – cut Margaret's line) *Much Ado About Nothing*
> **Desdemona** (1.3 – from 'My noble father ... the Moor my lord' then add 'That I did love the Moor'; 4. 2) *Othello*
> **Lady Anne** (1.2; 4.1) *Richard III*
> **Juliet** (2.2; 2.5; 3.2; 4.3) *Romeo and Juliet*
> **Miranda** (3.1 – cut Ferdinand's lines) *The Tempest*
> **Silvia** (4.3) *Two Gentlemen of Verona*
> **Hermoine** (3.2) *The Winter's Tale*
> **Perdita** (4.6) *The Winter's Tale*

Nymphadora Tonks – *an 'outsider' sort of heroine – makes and follows her own rules, but once she decides what is right she's brave enough to put her heart on the line. A good hearted person, she's changeable, can be unpredictable, sometimes reckless and impulsive. Juvenile or Young Adult. Good for actors comfortable playing characters who are: confident and vulnerable, with tendency to display emotion carefully or reservedly in social circumstances. Driven by worldly or spiritual passion and desire.*

> **Helena** (1.1; 1.3; 3.2) *All's Well That Ends Well*
> **Rosalind** (3.2; 3.5; 5.2) *As You Like it*
> **Joan La Pucelle** (1.2; 3.3; 5.3) *Henry VI, Part 1*
> **Eleanor, Duchess** (1.2 [can cut and paste]; 2.4) *Henry VI, Part 2*
> **Lady Percy** (2.3) *Henry IV, Part 2*

Beatrice (4.1 – 'Is he not approved …' to 'woman with grieving' – cut Benedick's lines) *Much Ado About Nothing*
Helena (1.1; 2.2; 3.2) *Midsummer Night's Dream*
Juliet (2.2; 2.5; 3.2; 4.3) *Romeo and Juliet*
Katharina (4.3; 5.2) *Taming of the Shrew*
Cressida (1.2; 3.2) *Troilus and Cressida*
Emilia (1.3; 3.6; 4.2; 5.1) *Two Noble Kinsmen*
The Jailer's Daughter (2.4; 2.6; 3.2) *Two Noble Kinsmen*

Luna Lovegood – *quirky character – strong, wise, off-beat and a bit of a loner. Interested in things that others might not notice. She's brave and willing to put up a fight when necessary, even when no one else agrees with her or sees her point of view. Juvenile or Young Adult. Good for actors comfortable playing characters who are: Confident, injured, instinctive and tend to display emotion freely. Driven by passion, curiosity and a desire to control.*

Phebe (3.5) *As You Like it*
Joan La Pucelle (1.2; 3.3; 5.3) *Henry VI, Part 1*
Helena (1.1; 2.2; 3.2) *Midsummer Night's Dream*
Katharina (4.3; 5.2) *Taming of the Shrew*
The Jailer's Daughter (2.4; 2.6; 3.2) *Two Noble Kinsmen*

Bellatrix Lestrange – *a warrior: strong, will seem evil and heartless to anyone not affiliated with her 'tribe', beautiful, passionate and dangerous. She's willing to risk anything in her own cause, and has no fear of what the world might think of her. She's restless and has a very dark side. Young Adult/Mature. Good for actors comfortable playing characters who are: decisive, confident, entitled, with a tendency to display emotion freely or even extravagantly. Driven by desire and the need to control.*

Cleopatra (1.5 – very short; 2.5 – from 'Oh that his fault …' – cut Charmian's lines; 5.2) *Antony and Cleopatra*
Volumnia (1.3; 3.2 – cut Menenius' line; 5.3) *Coriolanus*
Queen (1.5; 3.1) *Cymbeline*
Eleanor, Duchess (1.2 [can cut and paste]; 2.4)

Henry VI, Part 2
Joan La Pucelle (1.2; 3.3; 5.3) *Henry VI, Part 1*
Queen Margaret (1.3; 3.1) *Henry VI, Part 2*
Queen Margaret (1.1 & 4; 3.3 [cut King Lewis]; 5.4; 5.5 [cut Edward & Clarence]) *Henry VI, Part 3*
Goneril (1.3 – cut Oswald's lines; 1.4; 4.2 – cut Edmund's line) *King Lear*
Hecate (3.5) *Macbeth*
Lady MacBeth (1.5; 1.7 – cut Macbeth's line) *Macbeth*
Queen Margaret* (1.3, 4.4) *Richard III*
Tamora (1.1; 2.2 or 3, depending on edition) *Titus Andronicus*

Rita Skeeter – *sexy, authoritative, mischievous, wily and worldly. She gets what she wants and isn't afraid. Her confidence – even in the worst of circumstances – makes her hard to resist. Young Adult or Mature. Good for actors comfortable playing characters who are: decisive, confident, extroverted, with tendency to display emotion freely or extravagantly. Driven by desire.*

Cleopatra (1.5 – very short; 2.5 – from 'Oh that his fault ...' cut Charmian's lines; 5.2) *Antony and Cleopatra*
Luciana (3.2) *Comedy of Errors*
Gertrude (4.7) *Hamlet*
Constance (2.2 [sometimes listed as 3.1]; 3.3 [sometimes listed at 3.4) *King John*
Mistress Ford (2.1) *Merry Wives of Windsor*
Mistress Page (2.1) *Merry Wives of Windsor*
Titania (2.1; 3.1 – cut Bottom's lines) *Midsummer Night's Dream*

Dolores Umbridge – *despite (possibly motherly) appearance, she has a steely determination to have her way in all things. She is good at hiding her true nature and will do anything in the service of her own cause. Good for actors comfortable playing characters who are: decisive, manipulative, empowered, with varied tendency to display emotion – anywhere from reserved to extravagant. Driven by the need to control or to right injustice.*

Queen Katherine (2.4; 3.1 – cut Wolsey's latin line in first mono, cut Campeius' line in second mono; 4.2 – cut Capucius' lines) *Henry VIII*
Constance (2.2 [sometimes listed as 3.1]; 3.3 [sometimes listed as 3.4) *King John*
Queen Margaret* (1.3; 4.4) *Richard III*

Men

Young Harry Potter – *strong all round leading action hero: rather innocent in the ways of the world, compassionate, brave but also has a share of humility and sometimes thinks more of the welfare of others than himself. Can be obsessed by a single cause or injustice and willing to risk anything to make things right. Juvenile or Young Adult. Good for actors comfortable playing characters who are: Decisive, independent, vulnerable, injured, with tendency to display emotion freely. Driven by curiosity and desire.*

    Orlando (1.1; 2.7 – cut Duke Senior's line) *As You Like it*
    Antipholus of Syracuse (3.2) *Comedy of Errors*
    John Talbot (4.5 – cut two lines of Talbot Sr.'s) *Henry VI, Part 1*
    Prince Hal (4.5; 5.3) *Henry IV, Part 2*
    Boy (3.2) *Henry V*
    Hotspur (1.3; 2.3; 3.2; 4.3) *Henry IV, Part 1*
    Young Clifford (5.2) *Henry VI, Part 2*
    Berowne (1.1; 3.1; 4.3; 5.2) *Love's Labours Lost*
    Benedick (2.1; 2.3) *Much Ado About Nothing*
    Romeo (2.2; 3.3; 5.1; 5.3) *Romeo and Juliet*

Older Harry Potter – *strong all round leading action hero: has grown wiser, remains compassionate and brave, but is increasingly isolated by his own obsessions and is somewhat uncommunicative. A 'complex' hero, who carries the burdens of many others. Juvenile or Young Adult. Good for actors comfortable playing characters who are: decisive, independent, injured with a tendency to suppress emotion or display reservedly. Driven by a desire for justice.*

Hamlet (1.2; 1.4; 2.2; 3.1; 3.3; 3.4; 4.4) *Hamlet*
Prince Hal (4.5; 2.2) *Henry IV, Part 2*
King Henry (1.2; 2.2; 3.1, 3 and 6; 4.1, 3, and 8; 5.2) *Henry V*
Talbot (1.4; 1.5; 4.6) *Henry VI, Part 1*
Brutus (2.1; 3.2) *Julius Caesar*
Antony (3.1; 3.2) *Julius Caesar*
Lennox (3.6) *Macbeth*
Malcolm (4.3) *Macbeth*
Richmond (5.3; 5.5) *Richard III*
Troilus (2.2) *Troilus and Cressida*

Ron Weasley – *somewhat awkward; more a follower than a leader. May have more or less observable personality than typical 'hero' or leading man type but brave, reliable, fiercely loyal and willing to serve others. He has a quietly practical nature and is something of an 'everyman' in extraordinary circumstances. Juvenile or Young Adult. Good for actors comfortable playing characters who are: vulnerable, trusting and social. Tendency to display emotion either freely, and driven by a need for approval and/or social harmony and justice.*

Antipholus of Ephesus (5.1) *Comedy of Errors*
Pisanio (3.2; 3.4 – cut Imogen's line and 'Well then, here's the point') *Cymbeline*
Horatio (1.1) *Hamlet*
King Henry (4.1; 5.5) *Henry VI, Part 1*
King Henry (3.1) *Henry VI, Part 2*
King Henry (2.5; 3.1; 5.6) *Henry VI, Part 3*
Edgar (2.3; 4.6; 5.3 – cut Edmund and Albany lines) *King Lear*
Salerio (1.1) *Merchant of Venice*
Lorenzo (5.1) *Merchant of Venice*
Aeneas (1.3) *Troilus and Cressida*

Lucius Malfoy – *strong character: quiet, sinister. An arrogant warrior, capable of powerful things. Rebellious and loyal to his own cause at any cost. Has unshakeable conviction, which makes him relatively fearless. But there is a strain of mysterious complexity about him that gives him a sense of torment. Young Adult/Mature. Good for actors comfortable playing characters who are: decisive, entitled, and cautious, with a* *tendency to suppress emotion. Driven by desire for power and a need to control.*

Coriolanus (1.1; 2.3; 3.1; 4.1; 4.5; 5.3) *Coriolanus*
Iachimo (2.2; 5.5) *Cymbeline*
Claudius (1.2; 3.3; 4.5) *Hamlet*
Westmoreland (4.1) *Henry IV, Part 2*
Lancaster (4.2) *Henry IV, Part 2*
Suffolk (5.3; 5.5) *Henry VI, Part 1*
Hume (1.2) *Henry VI, Part 2*
Richard Duke of Gloucester (3.2; 5.6) *Henry VI, Part 3*
Pandulph (3.1; 3.3 or 4 – depending on edition – can cut Lewis' line) *King John*
Lewis the Dauphin (5.2) *King John*
Edmund (1.2, 2.1 – cut Gloucester's line) *King Lear*
Macbeth (1.7; 2.1; 3.1) *Macbeth*
Angelo (2.1 – cut Escalus' line; 2.2; 2.4 – cut Servant's line and 'Teach her the way) *Measure for Measure*
Iago (1.3; 2.1; 2.2; 2.3) *Othello*
Richard (1.1; 1.2; 2.1; 3.5; 3.7; 4.4; 5.3) *Richard III*
Saturninus (4.4) *Titus Andronicus*

Albus Dumbledore – *wise, strong leader who has commanding authority even in the face of his enemies. Can be whimsical or eccentric and display a wry sense of humour, but has a great store of courage and intellectual curiosity. Mature. Good for actors comfortable playing characters who are: decisive, vulnerable, authoritative, ambiguous, with a tendency to suppress emotion. Driven by desire to right injustice in the world.*

The King (1.2; 2.3) *All's Well That Ends Well*
Jaques* (2.7) *As You Like it*
Aegeon (1.1) *Comedy of Errors*
Menenius Agrippa (2.1; 5.2) *Coriolanus*
Cominius (2.2) *Coriolanus*
Belarius (3.3; 5.5) *Cymbeline*
Ghost* (1.5) *Hamlet*
Duke of Burgundy (5.2) *Henry V*

Mortimer (2.5) *Henry VI, Part 1*
Earl of Worcester (5.1; 5.2) *Henry IV, Part 1*
Shylock* (1.3; 3.1; 4.1) *Merchant of Venice*
Antonio (4.1) *Merchant of Venice*
Leonato (4.1; 5.1) *Much Ado About Nothing*
Friar Francis (4.1) *Much Ado About Nothing*
John of Gaunt* (2.1) *Richard II*
Bishop of Carlisle (4.1) *Richard II*
Prince (1.1) *Romeo and Juliet*
Prospero* (1.2 – cut Miranda's lines; 5.1) *The Tempest*
Theseus (1.4; 5.3; 5.4) *Two Noble Kinsmen*

Sirius Black – *the 'troubled' hero; brave and dark and sometimes sinister, fiery, obsessive, but deeply loving. He can be edgy and rebellious, but ultimately craves a just world where he can be accepted for exactly who/what he is. Young Adult or Mature. Good for actors comfortable playing characters who are: vulnerable, instinctive, ambiguous, injured, with tendency to display emotion freely or even extravagantly. Driven by desire to control or to right injustice.*

Antony (1.2; 4.12, 4.14) *Antony and Cleopatra*
Coriolanus (1.1; 2.3; 3.1; 4.1; 4.5; 5.3) *Coriolanus*
Hamlet (1.2; 1.4; 2.2; 3.1; 3.3; 3.4; 4.4) *Hamlet*
Laertes (1.3) *Hamlet*
Prince Hal (1.2; 2.4; 3.2; 5.4) *Henry IV, Part 1*
Hotspur (1.3; 2.3; 4.1 – cut Worceser's line, 4.3) *Henry IV, Part 1*
King Henry (1.2; 2.2; 3.1, 3 and 6; 4.1, 3, and 8; 5.2) *Henry V*
Constable of France (4.2) *Henry V*
Warwick (3.2) *Henry VI, Part 2*
Duke of York (1.1; 3.1) *Henry VI, Part 2*
Duke of York (1.4) *Henry VI, Part 3*
Warwick (2.1; 4.2; 5.2) *Henry VI, Part 3*
Clifford (2.2; 2.6) *Henry VI, Part 3*
Duke of Buckingham (1.1; 2.1) *Henry VIII*
Brutus (2.1; 3.2) *Julius Caesar*
Antony (3.1; 3.2) *Julius Caesar*
Philip the Bastard (1.1; 2.1; 5.2) *King John*
Othello (1.3; 3.3; 5.2) *Othello*

Richard II (1.3; 3.2; 3.3; 4.1; 5.5) *Richard II*
Macbeth (1.7; 2.1; 3.1) *Macbeth*
Claudio (1.2 – cut Lucio's line and 'Unhappily, even so'; 3.1 – cut Isabella's line) *Measure for Measure*
Prince (1.1) *Romeo and Juliet*
Lucius (5.3) *Titus Andronicus*
Troilus (2.2) *Troilus and Cressida*

Severus Snape – *strong character: sarcastic, sometimes unreadable, sinister and ultimately more vulnerable than he looks. He may be a good man with evil tendencies or an evil man with good tendencies. He is extremely complex and his actions are often hard to interpret immediately. Young Adult or Mature. Good for actors comfortable playing characters who are: ambiguous, injured, dangerous, self-entitled, and introspective, with a tendency to suppress emotion. Driven by a desire to control or to right an injustice.*

Oliver (1.1; 4.3) *As You Like it*
Tullus Aufidius (4.5; 4.7) *Coriolanus*
Archbishop (1.3; 4.1) *Henry IV, Part 2*
King Henry (1.1; 3.2) *Henry IV, Part 1*
King Henry (3.1; 4.4; 4.5) *Henry IV, Part 2*
King John (2.1; 3.3; 4.2 – cut Hubert's line) *King John*
King Philip (2.1; 3.1) *King John*
Macbeth (1.7; 2.1; 3.1) *Macbeth*
Brabantio (1.2) *Othello*
Bolingbroke (1.1; 2.3; 3.1; 3.3) *Richard II*
Mowbray (1.1; 1.3) *Richard II*
Duke of York (2.1, 2.2) *Richard II*
Buckingham (3.7) *Richard III*
Ulysses (*Troilus and Cressida*)
Bolingbroke (1.1; 2.3; 3.1; 3.3) *Richard II*
Marcus (1.1; 2.2 or 3 – depending on edition) *Titus Andronicus*
Ulysses (1.3; 3.3) *Troilus and Cressida*
Duke (3.1) *Two Gentlemen of Verona*

Peter Pettigrew – *strong and very quirky character; colourful, unreliable, may be a joker. Although generally loyal, he is always* *ultimately self-serving and often jealous of others. Jealousy may drive him to make bad decisions, or just seem rather unapproachable. Young Adult or Mature. Good for actors comfortable playing characters who are: ambiguous, vulnerable, disruptive with a tendency to display emotion freely. Driven by desire for power, control or approval.*

Cloten (4.1) *Cymbeline*
Armado (1.2; 5.1) *Love's Labour's Lost*
The Porter (2.3) *Macbeth*
Falstaff (3.5; 4.1) *Merry Wives of Windsor*
Ford (2.2; 3.2) *Merry Wives of Windsor*
Egeus (1.1) *Midsummer Night's Dream*
Thersites (2.3; 5.1; 5.4) *Troilus and Cressida*
Malvolio (2.5; 3.4) *Twelfth Night*
Trinculo (2.2) *The Tempest*
Autolycus (4.4) *The Winter's Tale*

Cedric Diggory – *intelligent, honest, loyal, brave, trustworthy. A warrior who follows, but not a leader. In different times, he may have been a leader, but he is surrounded by strong personalities who command. May have a strong romantic streak, but it isn't his most noticeable trait. Juvenile, Young Adult or Mature. Good for actors comfortable playing characters who are: social, trusting, and decisive, with tendency to suppress or be cautious about displaying emotion. Driven by passion and the desire to serve.*

Exeter (2.4; 4.6) *Henry V*
Montjoy (3.6) *Henry V*
Salisbury (1.1; 3.2) *Henry VI, Part 2*
Malcolm (4.3) *Macbeth*
Bassanio (1.1 – cut Antonio's line; 3.2) *Merchant of Venice*
Hector (2.2; 4.5) *Troilus and Cressida*
Sebastian (4.3) *Twelfth Night*
Palamon (2.2; 3.6; 5.1) *Two Noble Kinsmen*
Arcite (2.2; 2.3; 3.1; 5.1) *Two Noble Kinsmen*

Neville Longbottom – *socially awkward, perhaps a late-blooming hero who has a powerful sense of right and wrong, which gives him* *courage at times. He is an introverted character who blossoms in dangerous situations. Loyal and self-effacing. Juvenile or Young Adult. Good for actors comfortable playing characters who are: vulnerable, self-sacrificing, and trusting, with a tendency to suppress emotion. Driven by a desire for harmony, justice and social order.*

> **King Henry** (4.1; 5.5) *Henry VI, Part 1*
> **King Henry** (3.1) *Henry VI, Part 2*
> **King Henry** (2.5; 3.1; 5.6) *Henry VI, Part 3*
> **Malcolm** (4.3) *Macbeth*

Arthur Weasley – *hard working, loving, loyal, good-hearted and brave, when called upon. Not a leader, but a strong team member. Willing to be self-sacrificing for the right cause. Young Adult or Mature. Good for actors comfortable playing characters who are: Vulnerable, social, trusting, and self-effacing, who tend to display emotion carefully. Driven by desire to serve.*

> **Polonius*** (1.3) *Hamlet*
> **King Henry** (4.1; 5.5) *Henry VI, Part 1*
> **King Henry** (3.1) *Henry VI, Part 2*
> **King Henry** (2.5; 3.1; 5.6) *Henry VI, Part 3*
> **Friar Francis** (4.1) *Much Ado About Nothing*
> **Friar Laurence** (2.3; 3.3; 4.1; 4.5; 5.3) *Romeo and Juliet*
> **Pirithous** (4.2; 5.4) *Two Noble Kinsmen*
> **Antigonus** (3.3) *The Winter's Tale*
> **Polixines** (4.2) *The Winter's Tale*

Hagrid – *an awkward outsider, loyal and slightly rebellious at the same time. An earthy humanity and good sense of humour. Utterly loyal to his own cause and can be fiercely loyal to others he has 'adopted' or who have earned his respect. Young Adult or Mature. Good for actors comfortable playing characters who are: Vulnerable, social, trusting, and extroverted. Tendency to display emotion freely. Driven by desire for approval.*

> **Menenius Agrippa** (2.1; 5.2) *Coriolanus*
> **Falstaff** (2.2; 2.4) *Henry IV, Part 1*

Falstaff (1.2; 3.2; 4.3; 5.1) *Henry IV, Part 2*
Boyet (5.2) *Love's Labour's Lost*
Launcelot Gobbo (2.2) *Merchant of Venice*
Bottom (4.1) *Midsummer Night's Dream*
Biondello (3.1) *Taming of the Shrew*
Nestor (1.3) *Troilus and Cressida*
Pandarus* (5.11) *Troilus and Cressida*
Launce (2.3; 4.4) *Two Gentlemen of Verona*

Fred or **George Weasley** – *disruptive, funny, creative character who can't quite be comfortable in traditional roles or settings. These characters find it hard to accept authority and always have their own very unique take on the world. Affable and loyal to those who have earned their respect. Juvenile, Young Adult or Mature. Good for actors comfortable playing characters who are: social, instinctive, decisive and self-entitled, who display emotion freely. Driven by curiosity and passion.*

Parolles (1.1 – cut one or 2 lines of Helena's) *All's Well that Ends Well*
Touchstone (3.3; 5.4) *As You Like it*
Antipholus of Syracuse (3.2) *Comedy of Errors*
Hotspur (1.3; 2.3; 4.1 – cut Worceser's line, 4.3) *Henry IV, Part 1*
Prince Hal (1.2; 2.4; 3.2; 5.4) *Henry IV, Part 1*
Falstaff (2.2; 2.4) *Henry IV, Part 1*
Falstaff (1.2; 3.2; 4.3; 5.1) *Henry IV, Part 2*
Boy (2.2) *Henry V*
Berowne (1.1; 3.1; 4.3; 5.2) *Love's Labour's Lost*
King of Navarre (1.1; 2.1) *Love's Labour's Lost*
Lucio (1.4) *Measure for Measure*
Fenton (4.6) *Merry Wives of Windsor*
Gratiano (1.1) *Merchant of Venice*
Launcelot Gobbo (2.2) *Merchant of Venice*
Oberon (2.1; 3.2; 4.1) *Midsummer Night's Dream*
Benedick (2.1; 2.3) *Much Ado About Nothing*
Mercutio (1.4; 3.1) *Romeo and Juliet*
Petruchio (4.1; 4.3) *Taming of the Shrew*
Lucentio (1.1) *Taming of the Shrew*
Trinculo (2.2) *The Tempest*

Launce (2.3; 4.4) *Two Gentlemen of Verona*

Remus Lupin – *dark, loyal, thoughtful and loving, but a seriously tortured soul. Wants desperately to be good, sometimes can't. Although he is fundamentally a good person, he has secrets or obsessions that sometimes drive him off the rails. A fierce warrior who isn't above deception in the pursuit of his own cause. Young Adult or Mature. Good for actors comfortable playing characters who are: vulnerable, injured and instinctive, who display emotion freely if sometimes rather cautiously. Driven by passion and sense of duty.*

Domitius Enobarbus (2.2 – cut Agrippa's line) *Antony and Cleopatra*
Coriolanus (1.1; 2.3; 3.1; 4.1; 4.5; 5.3) *Coriolanus*
Tullus Aufidius (4.5; 4.7) *Coriolanus*
Posthumus Leonatus (2 4 or 2.5 in some editions; 5.1; 5.3; 5.4) *Cymbeline*
Prince Hal (1.2; 2.4; 3.2; 5.4) *Henry IV, Part 1*
Duke of Gloucester (1.1; 3.1) *Henry VI, Part 2*
George, Duke of Clarence (5.1) *Henry VI, Part 3*
Earl of Worcester (5.1; 5.2) *Henry IV, Part 1*
Cardinal Wolsey (1.2; 2.4; 3.2) *Henry VIII*
King Henry (2.4) *Henry VIII*
Cassius (1.2; 1.3) *Julius Caesar*
Hubert (2.1 [sometimes attributed to 'First Citizen']) *King John*
Salisbury (5.2) *King John*
Melun (5.3 or 4, depending on edition) *King John*
King Lear* (1.1; 2.2; 3.2; 4.6) *King Lear*
Albany (4.2 – cut Goneril's line) *King Lear*
Duke Vicentio (1.3; 3.1; 3.2; 3.3)
Shylock* (1.3; 3.1; 4.1) *Merchant of Venice*
Borachio (5.1) *Much Ado About Nothing*
Pericles (1.1; 1.2) *Pericles, Prince of Tyre*
Bolingbroke (1.1; 2.3; 3.1; 3.3) *Richard II*
Stanley, Earl of Derby (5.3) *Richard III*
King Edward (2.1) *Richard III*
Clarence (1.4) *Richard III*
Capulet (1.2; 3.5) *Romeo and Juliet*

Proteus (2.4; 2.6) *Two Gentlemen of Verona*
Leontes (1.2; 5.1; 5.3) *The Winter's Tale*

Voldemort – *evil and openly so. Can be seductive and charming when necessary but completely untroubled by killing others to gain power. Psychopathic-type villain, who has no concept of the needs or the pain of others. He relishes his own destructive power. Juvenile, Young Adult or mature. Good for actors comfortable playing characters who are: vulnerable, dangerous and injured, who tend to suppress emotion. Driven by desire for power and need to control.*

Iago (1.3; 2.1; 2.2; 2.3) *Othello*
Richard (1.1; 1.2; 2.1; 3.5; 3.7; 4.4; 5.3) *Richard III*
Titus Andronicus (1.1; 3.1; 3.2; 4.3; 5.2) *Titus Andronicus*
Aaron (2.1; 2.3; 4.2; 5.1) *Titus Andronicus*
Achilles (3.3) *Troilus and Cressida*

Gilderoy Lockhart – *bright, vain and utterly self-serving. Happy to put himself forward, even knowing his own shortcomings. His vanity can lead him to harm others, simply because he is so self-absorbed he doesn't see the whole picture. Can be very charming and successful in spite of all that. Juvenile, Young Adult or Mature. Good for actors comfortable playing characters who are: selfish, vulnerable, instinctive, and ambiguous, who tend to display emotion freely. Driven by desire or approval.*

Antipholus of Ephesus (5.1) *Comedy of Errors*
Iachimo (2.2; 5.5) *Cymbeline*
Cloten (4.1) *Cymbeline*
Hotspur (1.3; 2.3; 4.1 – cut Worceser's line, 4.3) *Henry IV, Part 1*
Suffolk (5.3; 5.5) *Henry VI, Part 1*
Suffolk (3.2) *Henry VI, Part 2*
Cardinal Wolsey (1.2; 2.4; 3.2) *Henry VIII*
Berowne (1.1; 3.1; 4.3; 5.2) *Love's Labours Lost*
King of Navarre (1.1; 2.1) *Love's Labour's Lost*
Fenton (4.6) *Merry Wives of Windsor*
Theseus (5.1) *Midsummer Night's Dream*
Benedick (2.1; 2.3) *Much Ado About Nothing*

Roderigo (1.1) *Othello*
Petruchio (4.1; 4.3) *Taming of the Shrew*
Richard II (1.3; 3.2; 3.3; 4.1; 5.5) *Richard II*
Mercutio (1.4; 3.1) *Romeo and Juliet*
Agamemnon (1.3; 2.3) *Troilus and Cressida*
Palamon (2.2; 3.6; 5.1) *Two Noble Kinsmen*
Arcite (2.2; 2.3; 3.1; 5.1) *Two Noble Kinsmen*
Proteus (2.4; 2.6) *Two Gentlemen of Verona*

Dobby – *not an elf, of course, but a good-hearted character who is an utterly humble and fiercely loyal servant. Not always able to see the bigger picture, and sometimes willing to deceive in order to serve. Juvenile, Young Adult or mature. Good for actors comfortable playing characters who are: vulnerable, trusting and self-sacrificing, with a tendency to suppress emotion. Driven by the desire to serve.*

Pisanio (3.2; 3.4 – cut Imogen's line and 'Well then, here's the point') *Cymbeline*
Polonius* (1.3) *Hamlet*
Canterbury (1.1; 1.2) *Henry V*
Friar Laurence (2.3; 3.3; 4.1; 4.5; 5.3) *Romeo and Juliet*
Antonio (5.1) *Twelfth Night*

'The extras'

Some monologues are spoken by characters who have limited roles (so little chance to determine their characteristics). This means that they might be played by any number of different character types. Some are not really written as human characters, and these monologues don't fit into a character type either, but you can judge whether they feel right for you by looking at the language or the balance of action to description:

Duke Solinus (1.1) *Comedy of Errors*
Balthazar (3.1) *Comedy of Errors*
Rumour (1.1) *Henry IV, Part 2*
Morton (1.1) *Henry IV, Part 2*
Lord Bardolf (1.3) *Henry IV, Part 2*

Chorus (Prologues, Acts 1–5) *Henry V*
Messenger (1.1) *Henry VI, Part 1*
Lieutenant or **Captain** (4.1) *Henry VI, Part 2*
Chatillion (2.1) *King John*
Murellus or **Murullus** (1.1) *Julius Caesar*
Morocco (2.7) *Merchant of Venice*
Arragon (2.9) *Merchant of Venice*
Puck (3.2) *Midsummer Night's Dream*
Lord (Ind. Sc) *Taming of the Shrew*
Ariel (3.3) *The Tempest*
2 Goth (5.1) *Titus Andronicus*

RESOURCES

Websites

www.shakespeareswords.com
This site was created by David and Ben Crystal, who are respected Shakespeareans. It has a lot of functions – you can find speeches, definitions, even whole plays. There is a lot of information here and many ways to explore it. You'll find it really helpful.

https://www.playshakespeare.com/
This site is incredibly helpful for actors. You'll find play summaries, character descriptions, monologues, scenes, apps, discussion boards, reviews, and much else.

http://www.shakespeare-online.com/
This site is a great resource when you want a lot of background on the plays. There's a glossary, summaries, and much historical and scholarly content. It is a rich and helpful site in all ways.

http://www.shakespeare-monologues.org/home
This site is a labour of love, built by actors for actors. It includes a vast store of monologues, and also includes monologues that have been 'stitched together' by cutting intervening dialogue, which means that you may find much more material here than you would expect.

http://shakespeare-w.com/english/shakespeare/terms.html
This site is entirely maintained by a Japanese 'bardophile' and is a truly enjoyable experience. It doesn't pretend to be an academic site – it is very clearly a 'fan' site. But there is a lot of good information here and this is a useful site if you want to dig deeper into literary terms and poetic meter. Has a large database as well.

http://internetshakespeare.uvic.ca
This is a more general site that brings together a massive number of links with Shakespeare information.

Speech analyzers

This is the link for a free downloadable version of UCL's WASP analyzer. I like this one because of the ease of readability and because it gives you a pretty clear indication of both intensity of sound and pitch range. You get a choice of graphs that it can display and I chose waveform and pitch. Here is the link for the download:

http://www.phon.ucl.ac.uk/resource/sfs/wasp.php

The picture it gives you is this:
I found it really easy to download and experiment with.

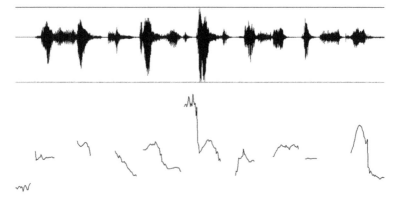

There is also a web application that allows you to play with sound and doesn't require a download. That's useful because it works with any system. It is super easy to use – hit record and then stop, and you'll get an immediate graphic of your sound. Here is the link:
http://www.speechandhearing.net/laboratory/wasp/

The picture it gives you is this:

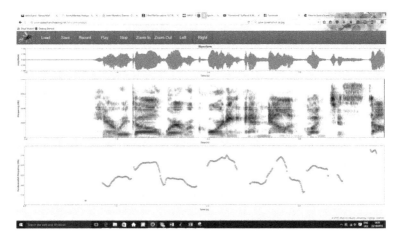

For those on a Mac operating system, the analyzer that I found was called Spectrogram Pro and you can find it for £2.99 on iTunes. There may be other, better software programmes out there, and if you have a Mac and you stumble onto one – please let me know. As you can see, the feedback from the two analyzers is very different – the Spectrogram Pro gives you this kind of visual:

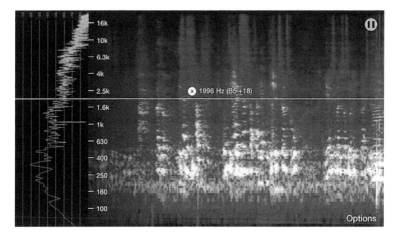

This actually looks much better in colour (as it will be on your screen). I prefer the clarity of the WASP, but I got used to gauging the Spectrogram Pro response and could certainly see the difference between my effort levels 1–10 when using it.

Books

Barton, John, *Playing Shakespeare* (London: Methuen, 2009).

Berry, Cicely, *The Actor and the Text* (London: Virgin Books, 2000).

Berry, Cicely, *Text in Action* (London: Virgin Books, 2001).

Block, Giles, *Speaking the Speech* (London: Nick Hern Books, 2013).

Carey, David and Carey, Rebecca, *The Vocal Arts Workbook and DVD: A Practical Course for Developing the Expressive Range of Your Voice* (London: Methuen, 2008).

Carey, David and Carey, Rebecca, *The Shakespeare Workbook and Video: A Practical Course for Actors* (London: Methuen, 2015).

Ewan, Vanessa and Debbie Green, *Actor Movement: Expression of the Physical Being* (London: Methuen, 2014).

Hall, Peter, *Shakespeare's Advice to the Players* (London: Oberon, 2014).

Houseman, Barbara, *Finding Your Voice* (London: Nick Hern Books, 2002).

Houseman, Barbara, *Tackling the Text* (London: Nick Hern Books, 2008).

Linklater, Kristin, *Freeing Shakespeare's Voice* (London: Nick Hern Books, 2010).

Rodenburg, Patsy, *Speaking Shakespeare* (London: Methuen, 2005).

Caliban - The Tempest

Peter Pettigrew
Malfoy?

1.30 ish

Lightning Source UK Ltd.
Milton Keynes UK
UKHW021819030122
396559UK00005B/588